TAXONOMIC VIGNETTES

TAXONOMIC VIGNETTES

Alan Cohen

atmosphere press

*To Maureen Neumann, for your interest and encouragement,
and to the friends who inspired these poems, all still cherished
for the joy and education you have given me.*

Contents

I. Irony of Promise

"Even now I can't see why it happens, the
moment of change,

but must try to witness each particular index

of landscape and irony of promise."

Dave Smith, "Messenger"
in *Goshawk, Antelope*

Confidence

1

He had always, as far back as he could recall
Suffered from prodigious skills and outsized ideas
And because nothing seemed beyond his reach
Would have to find a judicious balance between obscurity and
prominence
Choose a figure, cut a figure, in the world

Though man may well be the measure of some things
He saw that others are wholly beyond us
Though he himself could easily measure men
In a pinch, with spoon and tongs, insight and argument
And, for the most part, man did not measure up

So he decided that he could get away with it—make a virtue of his
quirks
Play at grandiose, at manic: Paul Bunyan, John Henry, Theseus
Embrace life like a centrifuge
And extract its critical elements
Live modest and unassuming on the supernatant

2

Without obsessions, without desires
He did what seemed right
Not dead center right of course, not square
Right up to a point, then chic, eccentric
In ironic vigor to deprecate the fates
* *

3

So was first in all his high school classes
But the only one in school to study Russian
(In honor of his crazy ancestors, those outsized Slavs
Karamazov, the czars, his father)
And a concert pianist; read Shakespeare, cover to cover, in tenth
                                        grade

Would quote from Henry VI and Timon of Athens during debates
Prom night played Tchaikovsky's concerto in Cleveland
Bespoke a voice like Orson Welles, cynosurial, commanding
For to be chic, might as well accept it, is to be arbitrary, a target,
                                        always at risk
A dandy not just in stance, dress, or word, but in deed

3

And so, right again, most right of all, he went to Harvard
Four years, graduated
But chic again, went into construction, became a foreman
Then right once more, to medical school
But still chic, a new one, with half days of classes

Regarding outcomes, life always has a winning hand
Even when we discount death
And life likes a good fight
Likes the young and the strong
Prefers, if not hubris, at least scope and confidence

It is comforting, this plenitude
This more than is needed
But to live out in the open, you must be able to go ten rounds with
                                        life

And then it turns out that's just the exhibition
It's more than 200,000 rounds, one for each day after childhood

4

He dripped with projects as a runner sweats
To found a private high school
Run for the senate, write an epic, visit the ocean floor
It was never ambition for money, fame, or power
Only thirst for a requisite challenge, to find an appropriate venue

School done, chose orthopedics; in time ran a big city ICU
Later, the Indian Health Service for a large state out West
Both right, perhaps, but neither chic enough
And so back to school, trained in management
Goal? To run a 1,200-bed hospital in Moscow

Meanwhile the biological clock was ticking
Pro-gen-y, dwel-ling, com-panion-ship
It was so hard to choose; he hesitated briefly
But then of course again chose what had always served
The difficult: the chic, upstanding, off-center right

5

And it started well
Married student housing
Trips to the mountains, picnics, camping out
Her world-class cooking: something different at every meal
The first child, a healthy son, within a year

* *

But that was the culmination of right and chic
She was, still is, Catholic and devout
Values humility and order
While he has always been liberal, uninhibited
Free of preference to this very fault

At first they deferred to one another
Both admirable, prodigious, appreciative
Meeting them, then, was glorious, transformational, transitory
They shone: such warmth, beauty, promise
Yet will alone could not suffice

6

We are, the best of us, mercifully resilient
Bend under squalls of chance and change
Endure, survive
But, predictably, bend only so far
And then spring back or break

Each prior choice had been time-limited
Contingent, on approval
While this one was final, irrevocable
Divorce is never chic or right
Especially with children

It taught him what he should have grasped before
It wasn't skills or strength that told
But being dead center right at crucial forks
Not chic, suspicious, careful, or considerate
But certain

In time they began to irritate and diminish one another
Well, once more knuckle down, nose to the grindstone, persevere,
                                    delay gratification
Another cross to bear, another river to cross
For appearances; to be responsible, fulfill commitments
And twenty years went by

Then life became impatient, intervened
Not once but twice
Cheated, some might say, stacked the deck
After all, children grown, they had already separated
He was already on his own again, still pinning hips, singing,
                            traveling with the symphony choir

So it may not have been impatience, but pique, contempt
Seeing mate now in three moves, at most five
The loss of another once worthy contender
In any case, there now followed: a massive heart attack, a coma
An ICU stay, near death for weeks

In recovery, life cleft
For the first time he wanted
Something he saw many others had
Wanted intimacy
Something that had never before signified
                    * *

Life's first incursion, coma, ICU, is easy to justify
"Heads up, reality check, you're not invincible, getting older"
But the second, the lymphoma, was tone-deaf, nasty
Life doing its thing because it can
His father had died young of lymphoma; now one year into his
                              second marriage, it invaded his wife

Yet, just as he has risen above every diurnal challenge
He has always also risen, floated above his life
Achieved far more of the quotidian than the average man, of all he
                              chose, suffered, conceived
A full participant, working extraordinarily hard, though that was
                              never the point
For he was never there in it really; but outside watching with an
                              ironic smile

9

And he has once again set me at odds with life, what he was and
                              deserved and got
Because for me that was heroism, his graceful and unassuming
                              exercise of talent
His perseverance beyond any reasonable expectation
I love the way he courted tragedy yet knew from the start
Just the right swerve to face it head on and still elude it at the last

"Honestly, though, I have no complaint
I'm no hero, never was
Life is more than fair and I love it
Have lived mine fully: two wonderful sons, and now a courageous
                              wife these fourteen joyous years
                    * *

Am completely satisfied, take my word"
My poem
His life/friendship
The way he wishes to be seen—or not

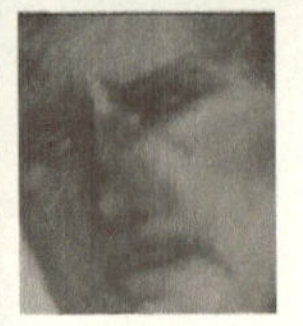

The Secret Life of Cover Art

1

Looking at the painting on this cover
I recall our fight
We wouldn't have called it that
A fight
But it was a bone serious difference
The kind that can end a marriage
"You don't want me to be successful," she said
"I don't want you to be disappointed," I said
It takes so many risks to make a successful marriage
But I digress

2

The cover art this morning
"Shooting Divas" by Pipilotti Rist (1996)
A Swiss artist, known for video installations
AKA Pipilotti (from Longstocking)
Trendy, my first thought
A woman's hand and flank
Two windows, shades mostly down, one snagged on a bias
A diaphanous gown
Only the hand rounded
So far, at least, a loose fit with the poems
But eye-catching
Disturbing in a David Lynch *Blue Velvet* way
Orange

10

3

The book, *Dance and Disappear* (2002)
Started it just this morning
Won the Juniper Prize
"Presented annually by the University of Massachusetts Press for a
                                        volume of original poetry"
Four poems in
Seems angry but energetic
More violence than joy
Little promise, much struggle
In a clear, strong, certain voice

4

M.'s was more sensuous, more colorful, more optimistic
Much happier with the world as it is
Its surprises, oddities
Even its disappointments
I Want This World (Tupelo Press, 2001)
MFA UMass
Read her poems out at our first gathering
The one in Belchertown in 1985
Her Ruby poems, her Polish poems
"Schermerhorn's Fish," "Zimpiceni's Marketplace"

5

She wanted "The Woman with Pots" for her cover
Anita's painting

That's what caused the turmoil
We were all thrilled and exultant when we agreed
But a week later
On the way to Pennsylvania, I think
I said "I hope you won't feel too bad if it doesn't happen"
I never could keep my mouth shut
But it did prepare her
And I do often seem to anticipate events
The publisher preferred Auguste Rodin's "Dancing Figure"
More famous, less specific
It's OK; "Woman with Pots," for *I Want This World*, was far better
We all knew

6

M.'s husband and I shared an office for ten years
At Medical West in Chicopee
Courtly, cautious, ironic, private
Immeasurably different, we liked and tolerated one another
He and M. had been to Africa with the Peace Corps
They had us to their annual Christmas Eve celebration
Introduced us to their friends
And came to all our gatherings
In our copy of *I Want This World*
She wrote "For two of my favorite friends and in celebration of
                                    our lasting friendship"

7

Anita designed the cover for *A Beast in a Cage of Words*
A book of poems about nuclear weapons I edited for PSR in 1985

First I called Leonard Baskin
He lived in Amherst, had collaborated with Ted Hughes
Was nasty, scathing
The only nice thing he said:
"Why don't you give young artists a chance?"
(Because your name would raise more funds)
I asked my wife

8

The last time we saw "Woman with Pots"
We were delivering it to an art lover in Illinois
Before we left for California
The last time we saw M.
She was on the couch beside A.
Quiet, confused, uncommunicative
We had been out of touch
Their daughter had gone off the rails
They had had lives full bringing her back
And then her own mind had begun to fail

9

"Life is hard," Anita often says
Though it's not how I think, she's right of course
Hard, ironic, even unkind
Alzheimer's for a poet in her fifties
A left-sided stroke (loss of speech)
For a marriage counselor
If art is defined by appreciation
Should the amount matter?

It's time for breakfast
The rain has stopped
Anita is cutting up the fruit
Waiting for me to make the coffee
Maybe we should call her husband again and commiserate
But we always run out of things to say, go quiet
And most books, I find, going back to the shelves
Have photos on their covers
Or graphic designs, classical paintings, sculptures
Most lives, I find, regress toward the mean
Still what we have made exists
Even if, as the song says, we can't always get what we want
And we find we need nothing

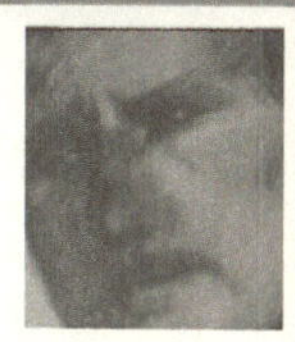

26

When Shadwell, the home he'd come into
When his father had died half his life before
Burned on February 1, 1770
Along with his legal briefs for the coming court session
His journals, and his library
No one was hurt
Twenty-six, he was already building Monticello
And he had outbuildings, other properties
Influential friends and slaves
To cushion the blow

But he wasn't insured
Granted continuances for most of his cases
He borrowed both books and the money to replace them
"These are gone," he wrote
"And like the baseless fabric of a vision
Leave not a trace behind."

A year later a "great fresh"
Destroyed the gristmill his father had left him
Along with its house and dam

Elected a burgess, he left the law
Moved into a single room across the river
And, first thing, planted fruit trees
Pears, apples, cherries, almonds, quinces, nectarines
Pomegranates, figs, walnuts, and apricots

Courted and married a widow
(Her only son died the summer before their New Year's Day wedding)
And moved her into his single room
While the building went on and on

These reverses now forgotten
We have our own scourges for this "Brother to Dragons"
Hold him to strict account
Drawing and quartering the quality of mercy

An Englishman, loyal to the crown
Looking south across the Rivanna
Or west to the Blue Ridge
His future unsettled
Single, shy, probably frightened
Despite his bravado
He didn't declare

He planned, hoped
Ventured his mind upon the world
Upon the future
Against long odds
As we, all of us alive, always must
Even now

Mentor

It's probably too late to start, Johnny-come, this now
You can no longer drift out to open the gate when we visit
Find it hard even to get from bed to chair
And so my access to you has changed: how you think, what you
                                          think about, what we can share
A year ago, two, you were still a familiar conundrum
A passionate Noam Chomsky or, better, Woody Guthrie radical
A serene Edward Weston photography enthusiast
A stubborn secular phenomenologist
Parsimonious in the drawing of conclusions
Now caught in an iron focus on physiological function
My fault entirely

You were the best teacher, the best mentor, I ever had
You emanated, radiated, what mattered most: love
Shy, mannered, wise, soft-spoken, humble
"No, no, thank *you*," you'd say, meaning nothing specific by it
Your personal, "Did you find everything OK?"
It should have been infuriating
Probably was for some
But to me it spoke volumes
Who you were, what you knew, what you felt you owed

I never wanted to attract attention
I am never sure enough of how, or if, to share what I know
I never acted upon a principle, but on hard, individual, irreducible facts
Afraid to overstep or overstate
My needs have been few, my life has been simple
Guided by curiosity and concern
I do love to share what I have learned

At least with those who are, like me, cautious and intent
But I have learned so little
In most respects I have remained a child

I didn't think to find you speaking here, in my poem
Like a deer in the forest, you've always been skittish, stood apart
So we've always met on neutral ground, ruled by such different minds
I learned, I thought I understood
But what was neutral was never solid. So, am I correct?
Most lives are in flight towards
But yours is in flight from
You left home and family, and learned cardiology all as armor, as a
                                defense
And at first that seemed—what was it you said?
An overstepping, an overstatement, passionate and absolute
As nothing else in your life has ever been

Well, yes, that is how I began, how I was launched
The energy that keeps me in stable orbit, in equilibrium
It sprang from my rejection of my family's way of life
Repulsion from cold WASP capitalism
Attraction to my warm Irish Catholic nanny
Once that was settled, I could see impartially, gather facts
Accumulate what would be useful
Set free by a conflict, resolved, incorporated in my DNA

So as you fled exploitation, fled Yale, money, fame, pride; stereotype,
                                definition
Fled even your nephew, Christopher Reeve
You lost some of your urgency, grew tranquil
Went surfing mornings, wore an aloha shirt, cutoffs and flip-flops
                                to the ICU

That silly endearing conspiratorial smile, the Right Guard
(Well, the odd bird still flew into the ICU then)
Could spend all day every day observing
We would sit, quiet afternoons, reading EKGs and nothing would
                                                    distract
It was all play, suggestion, proposal, and ideas about causes
"How do you think the PR interval might be affected by an
                                        opening snap?
Would it be longer, or perhaps shorter; might there be a dip and
                                        recovery in the P wave?"

Yes, it was the people that I knew, some famous now, some all along obscure
                                        as I am
And all those days by the bedside; each heart is an opportunity to learn
And the patients are so patient with us, welcoming, teaching
Those men whose discoveries made our work possible, mine and Fairy's, yours
No, no, and those women with heart failure, IHSS, endocarditis
They all suffered to make us proficient
That is what we owe
There is no urgency; everyday there are people in need
Everywhere, some in China, some next door
We can pay what we owe them a little at a time, on installment
Tranquilly, philosophically; not from guilt but in appreciation
There is, after all, nothing else worthy of our attention

But don't you dismiss too much?
Or have I just not lived quite long enough yet?
After all, there are people of good will everywhere
In commerce and teaching and government ("Yes, I agree")
I have to say that I liked Christopher Reeve ("Yes, so did I")
And there are departments and agencies
Libraries and theater companies and local governments

That act, address and invent like angels
Establish solid foundations, conceive visionary flights

I guess that's all true, but I can't say I trust institutions
Maybe it's just the disparity between large groups and small
But I long since decided to opt out, entirely out
I'd rather play guitar, go out to dinner, visit friends
Than listen to talking heads or politicians, to sales pitches, arguments, lies
In fifty years I haven't come across one I can stomach
That job doesn't seem to attract, to select for, anyone who would be truly good
at governing
It isn't the people: you can send off the best, but they change as soon as they're
underway

It's the rules, interpretations, institutions
But do you mind if we talk about Edward Steichen?
Or let me show you these algae that only grow in water over one hundred
degrees
I have a picture here, they're orange and they coat our hot-spring-fed pipes

If we're both deviants, both subversives, I perhaps less than you
Irritable thinkers, can't accept things as they are
But can't be satisfied with sublimation or escape
At least in our public lives (or in our embrace of Asian wives)
We do hold fast to native truths:
To loyalty, honor, kindness, leaving the world a better place
The way you kept going back to listen to that woman in heart
failure
(We all see thousands in the course of a career)
Listened at last, who can know why, on the right side of the chest
Found the continuous murmur all of us had missed, a rare AV fistula
And surgery cured her: an unsung deviant hero, at least for that day

* *

No, not a hero clearly, just lucky, just careful, don't you think
Anyone would do what I did; we all attend to our patients
Go back five or six times a day, as many as it takes if she's not better
Address one life at a time
I'm always impressed when you talk in large gestures
About all of humanity, laws and systems
Only revolution, a true turn of the wheel, can bring revelation
And that is far too large for me to foment or sanction
I myself, I can understand, can underwrite, can live with aiding one life at a time

So you stand apart, askance of the mainstream, out of the limelight
Seeking bank, pool, meander, oxbow
But whirlpools, eddies, countercurrents keep bringing you back to
                                        the center
You have lived now for twenty years at the top of the Napa Valley
In a hacienda on forty acres your wife's family bought in the 1960s
In the midst of wineries, pageantry, wealth
A mile from the geyser
You live here as in a garden or a desert
And of course you chose the old horse barn
As you once chose Kuakini, not Queens, then Kaiser, not UCSF
To pursue the accomplished anonymity you required

"..."

That's right, where we started.
You are almost gone now: we visit to honor you
It's the only ten-hour drive we find excuses to make
It may have been your fondest wish to be
The opposite of a spectacle:
Forgotten
But something stubborn about refusal and rightness

Persists, like an abstract sculpture at the center of a garden

A headland that divides incoming waves

History will celebrate Steven Sondheim, Willie Mays, Clint Eastwood,

Warren Buffett

Martin Luther King, Anne Frank, Harvey Milk, Mikhail Gorbachev

But I will celebrate you

Not an image, legend, or mystery

But the bare hard reality

Your humility, playfulness, and devotion

Your obscurity, love, and wisdom

Pleasant Street

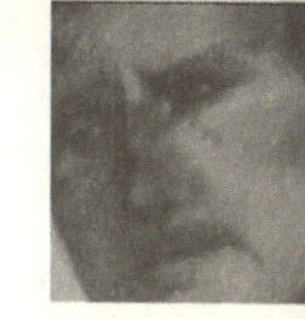

1

We met him at his theater
At a good time
For him
And for film in greater Northampton
Indie and foreign projections
(From Amherst, Calvin, Academy, and Pleasant Street Theaters
Amplifying the commercial fare at the Hadley, Holyoke, and
                                        Springfield malls)
He took tickets and greeted his customers
Outside both theaters
Upstairs Main, and downstairs Little
There pretty much whenever we visited
Open, sincere, knowledgeable, and kind
And with the least resources
Had the best programming

2

"I watched everyone burn out
In elementary, junior high and high school
College and medical school"
So said a friend who burned out
During his plastic surgery fellowship
But it wasn't just burning out
Some sold out
Some chickened out

Some dropped out
Some zoned out
Some bottomed out
Some reached their limit
Some became obsessed
Though in each case there was a common trajectory
A high point then a falling off
No second act
With him it was different

3

Probably the night the film billed for the Little Theater
Didn't arrive in time
And he asked, "Would you like to see *Una Giornata Particolare* instead?"
And we said, "Sure"
And were the only ones in the audience
Was when we crossed the border from client to friend

He was quietly becoming a local luminary
Business thriving, Ward 4 City Councilman
Soon to open an adjacent restaurant and video store
While we were just medical employees
But we shared world views and interests
With him and his wife
That year we coincided subscriptions to Hartford Stage
And the next they invited us to join their family
Them and their two daughters
At the Film Festival in Montreal

4

Of course America specializes in second and later acts
In might-have-beens and makeovers
And it's not just midlife crises
Or that half of our marriages end in divorce
Or that also-rans not infrequently become president
But also La Ronde
Doctor becomes lawyer
Lawyer politician
Politician priest
Priest hedge fund manager
Hedge fund manager doctor
Urban becomes rural
Sinner saint
Fool savant
Wannabe tycoon
And vice versa
But with him it was something else again

5

Thin mustache, symmetrical features
Valentino, Fairbanks, Depp
B stars, extras all came to mind
And the mind behind the features
Congenial, considerate, tranquil
To all appearances
At peace with himself and the world

First programmed movies during/for U Mass
Then taught and went on programming for nine years
Before opening Pleasant Street with his partner
And patiently building a reputation over another fifteen
Writing articles, networking, plying his trade
Attended Montreal as a journalist
Programmed for Boston and Hartford theaters
Met famous directors and actors
Producers and distributors

6

Perhaps the best measure of a man
The best test/trial/mark:
What he does when he gets what he wants
Spouse, job, first edition
Car, house, newspaper, satellite
Reach equilibrium
Or reach for something different
Something more

Was it for the sake of the thing
Or for the sake of the wanting?
What we become is a function of what we love
And what we do when we draw up alongside it
What is our love for?
Is it pain, appreciation, gratitude, longing?
Do we want it to stop?
Is it ours?
Perhaps the best measure of a man

Clearly he wasn't satisfied

7

The restaurant failed
Nor was it any longer a good time for cinema in the region
The Calvin closed
Amherst Cinema closed for renovation
And the Academy showing commercial films
DVDs and online ventures harrying the video store
He took on an eccentric project
Ghostwriting for what he called a Madam
(A not very prominent prostitute and her brothel)
Suddenly less accessible and more grandiose
No longer taking tickets
Or serving the city
He talked of opening a new business
Free of his partner
On Main Street
For movie memorabilia
Investing his net worth

Everyone he knew tried to dissuade him
"Not enough demand," "Too much risk"
It was like trying to convince the Niagara River
Not to descend into the Niagara Gorge
His mind made up
He was not willing to be confused by facts
But did want an audience for his debacle

8

As it happens, I also chose movies in college
At Vassar, junior and senior years

Selected the films that played each week on campus
From catalogs provided by the eminence grise
Who also did the ordering
I remained an amateur
A member of the audience
While she, like he, entered the business
After graduation worked in distribution at Paramount
Met Al Pacino, worked for him
Read lines with him on the set for Serpico
Spent years in film and TV
Then made a typical American transition
Took a Master's degree in history at UCLA
Wrote *Cuisine and Culture: A History of Food and People*
Now in its third edition
And *The Baking Powder Wars*
Definitely not the life for him; way too orthodox

9

So bet all his capital improbably
Painstakingly accumulated over twenty-five years
Of esoteric financial activity
On that single risky business venture
Which lasted six months
Then risked what remained of his life until then
Found a younger woman
Divorced
Left home, family, friends
Did drugs
Again did not fail overnight
Took another six months

To wash up alone, penniless, and chastened
But uncomplaining and unbowed in San Francisco
There simply to begin again

10

Any life can be upended between any two systoles
By what we call chance (the relatively unpredictable)
Heart attack, cancer, earthquake, pneumonia
Lightning, flood, mudslide, intimates' mishaps or deaths
Recession, stray bullet, misidentification
Or what we call choice (the relatively predictable)
Gambling, smoking, alcohol, venereal disease, extreme sports
Criminal, compulsive or obsessional acts
Most such pursuits personal, private, common, isolated
And, whatever the exposition, sudden
His was none of these

11

The impact of his unraveling
Was, like most such, rife
Some are pleased by and some sorry about
Any failure
Many, even on the periphery
Are more than one would anticipate affected
Of course his wife was devastated
Though sense and strength sustained her
His daughters had both by this time moved to San Francisco
The older was drinking heavily

And fell from a fourth storey roof
(This may have predated his demise
They shared demons, he and his oldest
Though his was more exacting
Hers more treacherous)
While his younger frankly throve
By the time he washed up at her door
She and her husband owned
The apartment in South SF he has lived in ever since
While rebuilding his life
And helping the older to recover hers

12

You know how electrons in molecules have energy levels
They are 2.3 microwhatevers or 3.45 from the nucleus
And require extra energy to change levels
The same seems to apply to sleep and weight
Four, six, and eight hours are my energy levels for sleep
Five or seven and I'm tired all day
And my weight settles in ranges 170-178, 178-185, 185-195
Vast extra effort required to move from one level to another
A patient once came to the office with heart and liver failure
Weighing 525 pounds
In hospital, he lost the water weight quickly
And after three weeks was down to 425
We sent him home to visit weekly
At 405 he literally disappeared
Phone calls, home visits, letters, police to his door
Nothing brought him back
Until his weight was back over 450 pounds

Our friend (don't ask why; he never let on)
Feels he deserves to be punished
There is no punishment without prior success
So he works hard for years
To achieve just the right degree of success
And then cannot be stopped
Until he has had sufficient punishment
At least that's how it looks to us

13

By the time we saw them again
The harshest misery and austerity were behind
And they had both rehabilitated
She could walk and work and enjoy her life again
And he was employed by the Mill Valley Film Festival
Was programming for an indie theater in San Rafael
After a short break again for Real Art Ways in Hartford
And episodically for other theaters on the East Coast
(Pleasant Street had closed once in 2007 and for good in 2012)
And his family had rallied back around him
Even his ex-wife visited now and again

We had moved to Fresno and for the next fifteen
Took him out to restaurants every two or three years
He'd aged and tamed, seemed progressively more tired
Less jaunty, less subversive
Acquired prostate cancer
Lost hair
I suppose we never knew him very well
Because it turned out he was only playing possum

In 2017, then 70, he was arrested for posting child pornography

online

In the longest letter we'd ever had from him

He explained he'd been researching a book

Like the one about the Madam

And he'd posted the photos as bait

To gather information from child pornographers

His ex-wife said the truth was much less clearcut

And we decided, as she had (temporarily, it turned out), we'd had

enough

He was convicted and went to jail for three years

But was released early courtesy of COVID-19

We find ourselves imagining that he is revving up once again

That it may be more difficult, just a greater challenge

And that if he lives long enough

He will have a third act

And presumably another still greater fiasco

If it's not in his genes

It's in his instincts and reflexes

He clearly feels he wants to have

But is not entitled to

Success

But can only relinquish it in nonconventional fashion

In a carefully choreographed public display

With just the right ambiance and trajectory

The precision of a jeweler, a cat, or a Jacques Rivette

Say in *Wuthering Heights* or *La Belle Noiseuse*

* *

About movies he was nearly always right
He introduced us to Rivette (not the man but his movies)
But about everyday life
He was stubbornly, helplessly wrong
So wrong and in such ways
That he was a threat and conundrum to himself
And to everyone who knew or cared for him
Though we must admit
That threat has not so far harmed us
Knowing him, for us, remains a net gain
And we plan to keep it that way

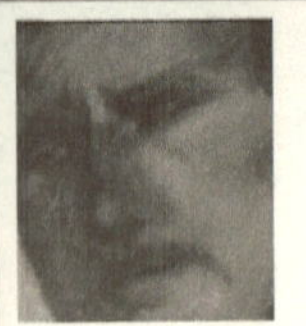

Fixed Smile

Waitress' smile
Elusive, proud
Then locals come in
Turns broad and coarse
Anything is not possible
Something is

Attachment

The first time I kissed a girl I loved I was twelve and swamped
by a hurricane of feeling I couldn't process or fathom which was
wonderful and terrible but what I didn't know was that I was kissing and in kissing helping to create a shadow someone just then
ceasing to exist solid as she was in my arms she I see now realized
kissing me she hated everything I was

It was the early sixties early May lilacs and crabapples and azaleas
all drenched in blossom sunny and breezy heady scents on the air
I'd just turned twelve the day before and she had come to *my* party
her gift words a life of Schweitzer a card love Linda and I trusted
words had wild hopes of them she'd been named best French student at school led cheers sang soprano in choir had a full frank
mouth and deep blue sparkling eyes probably no more idea yet
than I did she was going to leave all that behind

I conjured words conjured that birthday night what I felt what I
yearned for into a note that I gave her next afternoon at Joan's
party five houses from mine round the corner down the street
everything otherwise the same the sunlight the streamers the
crowd the outdoor grill hamburgers hot dogs roast beef beans
everything except what had passed between us and that made the
sky so intense my chest my arms so charged and watery it was
hard to eat hard to play parlor games hard to breathe

By then we'd had lots of parties spin the bottle truth or conse-
quences pecking kisses sweet ones but to be in a room alone her
sitting on my lap five minutes half an hour felt like half a year
rapt in fluid kisses that had no end was pure platonic bliss I not

* *

yet pubertal though she probably was and so kissing me was it
practice an experiment or was she just then as deluged as I but
sooner disenchanted

That was the last time I saw her a note had thriven I tried others
each seemed to make things worse school ended we went away for
the summer I sang "Sealed with a Kiss" accompanied by my tran-
sistor a thousand times by fall she'd abandoned words abandoned
propriety for a more earthy life squirrel's nest hair kohl-black eyes
slovenly clothes public displays of affection motorcycles demotic
speech slipped down a track rejecting among other things all that
I valued everything I was

I've always marveled at how people suddenly choose at seven or
twelve sixteen or twenty-five what they want to be attach them-
selves forcefully to a profession cult hobby study partner subcul-
ture discipline fashion change direction reject friends and family
build at great cost and effort something apt as this was for her
since it worked and at our reunion twenty-five years later she was
still defiantly that same chosen self and only the defiance gives
one pause she'd resolutely put the might-have-beens entirely
behind

While it seemed back then like only the two she'd had so many
choices so many attachments she might have formed or fled
could have been an actress feminist thief nun goth addict novel-
ist Muslim forest ranger any three could have moved to Montana
Paris Brazil rebellion can take so many forms at the time it did not
matter to me only that she was gone but now it's the choosing I
admire most the how and why and wish I could ask and she know,
share how much was genes family peers lovers reading disappoint-
ment promise fear that I looked to her perhaps like The Little

* *

Prince or Mister Magoo rejection of wealth education religion
cynicism goodness rejection begetting rejection acceptance begetting rejection something rich and strange always simmering in the
background so much ruthlessly left behind

II. Stubbornness of Character

"There is a stubbornness about me that never can bear to be frightened at the will of others. My courage always rises at every attempt to intimidate me."

Jane Austen, *Pride and Prejudice*

Dumb Blonde

Was I his?
It has taken me fifty years
To consider the possibility
I did always say:
"He was my best friend in high school"
Not
"We were best friends…"
I have no idea what he said
Or didn't

Don't know why we didn't meet sooner
Did he move late to the development?
Was he in a different track?
It seems almost as if he were
Someone fictional, someone I dreamed, imagined
Like a poem that I never got to write down
If it weren't for his etching on my wall
And his face there in the yearbook

Don't recall, either, how we became friends
Just one day were
And I had long-term close friends he displaced
There was about him something old and demonic
He seemed to know just what he wanted
Knew how the world worked
While I was slow to mature
Mutt and Jeff spring to mind. Laurel and Hardy
And yet not like them or anyone else at all
Snowflakes, unique in human experience
A historic mismatch

* *

He was funny
Didn't tell jokes
Made them up
Throwaways
I still use in conversation
"You're entitled to your opinion but you're wrong."
"Fun's a drag."
One day we went around our middle-class neighborhood
Door to door
"We're collecting for retarded children
If you have any just throw them in the bag"
Amoral, steely, an aesthetician
Didn't mind whom he offended
Or how he made his way
Yet charismatic, kind and thoughtful
Especially with friends
Vulnerable too, trusting
Ambiguous, various

I didn't know what gay was then
Hell, I hadn't even discovered marijuana
Played sports, collected stamps
Read comics, played board games
He was into shopping and music
Took me places I never would have gone
Played me Barbra Streisand (he, the Italian Catholic)
Introduced me to *We Have Always Lived in the Castle*
Of course I reciprocated
With Dickens and Keats
But all his bents were fresh and modern

* *

Yes, I saw he was effeminate
But to me that was just a trait, like his brown eyes
He was also forceful, clever and spontaneous
And, with him, so was I
We tormented poor F.M.
"Daddy, daddy, can you get us candy"
"I want that doggie"
F. just a classmate
Had made the mistake of joining us at the mall

He had lots of other friends
Male and female
I don't remember ever seeing him at school
But after school we were together often
Got to know each other's families, fears, and hopes
Quirks and preferences
Longings—at least the ones it was safe for us to share—
Each other's friends (we did not take to them)
Howard Johnson's, the beach
But he did not ride bicycles or play miniature golf or baseball
And I didn't go nightclubbing or dancing

The first nine months of college
Were the worst nine months of my life
And that summer back home
Absorbed in my first full time job
Sustained by family and friends, healing
Is, in memory, a blank succession of easy sunlit days
Broken only by one signal disruption
Which some people at parties still find the single most interesting
                                        thing about me

                        * *

When he proposed the trip upstate
I told him I didn't like live concerts all that much
But, when he persisted, showed me the poster
And I saw the Jefferson Airplane on the bill
I acquiesced
In the event only the three of us
He, me and his best female friend E. H.
Made the trip to Woodstock
With tent, sleeping bags, food, a Coleman stove
In my family's car

We didn't see the Jefferson Airplane
He got claustrophobic, insisted we leave
We did try but the car, as stubborn as any mule
Went only a hundred yards and then would not budge
AAA just laughed when we called for help
A local tow truck took us to the nearest town
But there would be no mechanic until Monday
My father had spent only one (in the family, celebrated) year
                              before the War outside NYC
In Jeffersonville, that nearest town
"Where no one ever locked their doors"
That was the only time I've been

I slept on a cot right out in front of the pumps
And walked around town in the morning without my glasses
Fuzzy morning glories, window boxes, cracked uneven sidewalk
Ghostly early risers out walking, companionable
It took the mechanic less than a minute
To find and fix the kink in the gas line
And later, that Monday evening,
We, together, on the radio, discovered Firesign Theatre

We'd been down our own private rabbit hole
And when we came back up
The waters around us had grown

I do not recall a single moment of sexual tension
Not a glance, not a sigh, not a touch
Not then, not ever
Perhaps, probably, as it has always seemed to me
We were just kindred spirits
Who loved one another's company
Rejecting convention, all we saw around us
Anarchic, happy, free
Or was I just oblivious
A big dumb blonde
And he an unrequited lover

Our high school principal was gay I later learned
One of our high school English teachers was too
But, I see now, not his kind of gay
They were coarse, gregarious, importuning
More Nathan Lane than Oscar Wilde
He was, when it came to taste
Severe, chic, inflexible
The etching on my wall is of Scott and Zelda
Black-and-white, linear, impersonal
Dated 1976, the year he suddenly lost weight
And no one knew why

The etching was a wedding present
Well first he tried to talk me out of marrying again
This time promoted *his* lifestyle
As if one might choose one's sexual preference

As from a menu a diet
A preventive health measure
A convenience
Knowing better, he then attended the wedding
Met and liked my wife
And went back to his life

By then he had also confided in me
About his days at the bank, his nights at the bathhouses
The fear and excitement
Told me how he stole downtown and sold uptown
Sweaters and scarves and such
To help make ends meet
He shrugged
A salary alone, he said, could not begin
To support a life in Manhattan

That was during his second remission
And by then his disease had a name
Too late to be safe and too soon for treatment
He was part of the target population
Helpless, in the sights of history
Like the generation that died on the beaches in Normandy
Of the 1919 influenza
During the Thirty Years' War
In the plague of the Thirteenth Century
At Hiroshima, in the camps
The Gulag, the Great Leap Forward
Once upon a time I would ponder what might have been
But now, more like him:
If my grandmother had had wheels
She'd have been a tricycle

* *

And I perhaps a school bus or tea caddy
Revisiting him though has returned to me
Images, fears and joys
Flickers of myself
Opened new ones
Restored the gyroscope
Of my comprehension
Because I had not earlier finalized or fixed
My sense of that early friendship
But left it hanging
I can now see it, place it
So much more deeply, fully, clearly
An emotional and semantic hologram
Hanging like a gibbous moon in my mind
Rather than just one more icon, ad, caricature or coin
Lost in one of the scrapbooks, habits or pockets
Of this aging, late blooming
Exceptionally slow, if not dumb, blonde

Warning Shot

When he awakens his heart is pounding
He's lived with this heart for 70 years
And it's never pounded like this before
It's always beat, never pounded
Whatever the emotion or provocation

Not even regular
And the stuttering
In contrast to the strong, staunch, slow, steady beat
Is a sentence
Or the breaking of one
A prophecy, a sign
Time short, limitations ahead
He'd been so proud of his regular heartbeat
So secure in it

Calls the doctor's office
Offered an appointment
Next day at ten
Checks with his wife
She's been unwontedly quiet
Mortality magnifying stealth and threat
Dwarfing words
Feeding and hiding their agitation
She nods
And he accepts
Still wondering if he should have insisted
He could be dead by tomorrow

* *

But then, once off the phone
He converts
Pulse steady again, wants to go sit in the sun
Meditate
But it's thirty-eight degrees out and raining
So he settles for a settee in the library
And settled, subtled, sees an image
Himself, with Sharon, in midair
Below him atom, molecule, cell, heart
Above neighborhood, community, state, country
The column swaying and, though threatening to collapse
Still upright

Next morning, in the office
Exam and EKG both normal
Heartbeat once more percussive and steady as a pile driver
He's reestablished on the Earth
Perhaps, he thinks, not two years ahead but twenty
Not reborn, not even rejuvenated
But reintegrated
Alive enough again to contemplate harness
And happiness

Therapist

1

Of course I can see now how he must have looked to others
Short, fat, arrogant, pushy, bourgeois
The kind of Jew I myself left Long Island to escape
Connected, grasping
Building a life by force of will
Unable to hold it together

But that was not the man I knew
That man was forthright, intrepid, idealistic, altruistic, masterful
An egotist but swashbuckling and fearless
We wrestled
We fought
About what life was for
How much one could give up, change
And still remain himself
About how to deal with pain
An inability to get a self to cohere
About desire and its satisfaction
About what is just and reasonable
About how to live in society

Yes, he was crass and infuriating
Stubborn and bombastic
But he respected the child I was
The adolescent I became
The man I'd one day be
And he saved me

2

He violated every code and standard
Treated my mother, brother, sister, and me
Not as a group, but one at a time
And met with us socially
At restaurants, at home
Split cases of wine from Sherry-Lehmann with my parents
Helped me buy an engagement ring

I will never know precisely
What his relationship was with my mother
Or how he felt about me
Nor does that, in retrospect, seem to matter
I did ask but never insisted
Never required lies or explanations
Thought in fact he had shared too much
Felt he had a right to privacy
That that served me, us

3

We knew he was divorced
Had four children
Was dragged back to court
Repeatedly
For amendments to the divorce decree
Was proud of his children, was lonely
Finally found a new partner
An aspiring actress
Someone we got to know quite well

51

Maybe better than he did
Who turned to us for advice and support
Both before his death and after

We knew that he taught at Albert Einstein
That he spoke German, had studied in Europe, was a Freudian
Embraced psychoanalysis
Saw each of us for an hour three times a week
Was usually conventionally silent, opinionless
As we, artfully urged, imparted
Thoughts and fears, and, especially, dreams
But would, at times, break ranks, intervene, pontificate
Provide interpretations, summaries
Which rarely rang entirely true
In an impenetrable sanctioned idiom
Portentous, rigid, improbable

IV

I spent the bulk of my childhood
Helpless and threatened
In my private city under bombardment
In a personal concentration camp of the imagination
Anticipating enemies, ogres
Blast, fire
Rough hands, a violent end
My mind was tuned to the wrong station
Miscalibrated
Not suited to this world
Needy, deserted
Starved for love, affection, relief from fear

No one's fault, born defective
My parents supportive, also helpless, anxious to help

He said he was taking risks
But did it with confidence
It was as if he spoke the program language of my mind
Rebooted, remapped it
Replaced the programming flaws
With the software that had been intended, needed
Dissected away the apocalyptic gothic imagery
It took, it seemed, forever, but once he'd intervened
The transition proceeded on its own
Year after year
Until one day I found myself free and open
Transported from hell all the way here

5

Any service can be bought
But the quality of any service
Is always a gift
His care, rare, was the best gift I ever got
Without the least loss of my earliest self
I was put back right
Never spent a day in hospital
Never took a single pill
I'd call it magic, fiction
If I had not been there

What he did
Not evidence-based, conventional or politically correct

(A mercy that he was not stopped, restrained)
I used to think that it could only have come from love
For me or us or anyway rightness
Though looked at another way
He did what he did because he had to
And it was in no way remarkable
Either way, he'd attained his condition of fire moment
To which one can only rise once
And which, to my mind, justified his life—
Amplified it
Reset its margins—
And, if there is one and he wished it, admission to heaven

This man at the peak of his powers
Giving all he had learned away
To some random family
Perhaps won forgiveness
For whatever in his life he'd done or was to do poorly
Falter/failing
Watching slip away
For just us
With strong arms and an open heart
In the sunlight, undismayed
Shining, mending, making

Best Poet Hands Down

1

And then he said
The best poet hands down
And I only discovered him a few years ago
A friend turned me on to him
And I've become not just a fan
An enthusiast
Is Jack Gilbert
You haven't read him
But if you haven't read him
You know nothing about poetry
The best book, of course, is the first one
Views of Jeopardy
But it's hard to come by
I got a copy back when
Nowadays it's a couple of thousand
On Amazon
And well worth it
You could probably start with Monolithos though
That will give you an idea of what poetry can be
And you'll still have a greater treat ahead in Views of Jeopardy

2

From ten to sixteen
My closest friends and I
Chose to spend
A substantial portion

Of our discretionary time
Perhaps ten percent, perhaps twenty-five
Four of us and only four
Exploring together
Crucial to one another

And then
The last two years of high school
He a fifth
Two years younger
Callow, ambitious, funny
With a demoniacal laugh
And a magpie's instinct for the shiny and new
A secular Jew like the rest of us
Was introduced
Took root, and grew
Did we condescend?
Was he resentful?

3a

Though some are partial to laughter
The opposable thumb
Burial or speech
Subscription
To a set or sets of values
Sequentially or simultaneously
Has always struck me
As what defines mankind
And I have always had
Near the top of my list

The things we freely choose
And at the very top of that
The people

Friendship is one such
A hard thing to define
Different I suspect for each of us
For me a free pass
Of my judgment
Won by virtu
By a set of values I recognize and applaud
But for others perhaps
A conditional pass for someone
Who pleases or protects or praises them

3b

Because in youth friendships overflow
Like fountains
In neighborhoods, at schools, at work
At camps, at meetings, during worship and sports
Every time one turns around
We have an impression of ease and abundance
But friendships require maintenance

Their gist
Their joy and purpose
Is time together
In person
Unhurried
Appreciation of each unique flavor

Each nuance of thought and gesture
Their beauty, artistry, awkwardness
Their distinctive conversational poetry

But this entails mechanics
Especially later in life
Staying in touch, setting aside time
Traveling
Maintaining a pilot light
An open place, a register
For the idiosyncrasy that is each friend
And few appreciate the value
Make the effort
Set aside the time
And so friends thin out

They change
No longer care
Are too busy with work and family
Are embarrassed by or miss who they once were
Or dislike what they've become
And don't want to be reminded
Get lazy, nasty, crotchety, old, pessimistic

4

So my first instinct
During that phone call
Our first contact in ten years
Was maintenance
To temporize and mollify

Promise to find and read Jack Gilbert
Work toward a face-to-face meeting
It might have been a bad week for him
Fights, bad news, illness, or injury
A blow to the ego
Who knew?
There might still be something worth saving

We'd been what we both called friends
Established a beach head
Meeting often
During the summers between college semesters
Before he left for Reed
And then, on a vacation from my first job
We visited his home in the hills above Portland
He met my wife and I met his
A Portland city planner
By then he was a food critic
Had his own column
Cooked us dinner

He was always sarcastic
Combative, competitive
But also funny
Full of energy
And he'd made it clear
From the start
He never wanted to work for a living
Wanted a work around
Found one
Thought those who worked nine to five
Thought me

Foolish

But enjoyed talking to me about it

5

So I visited Amazon

And *Views of Jeopardy* was indeed $2000

For the hardcover

But only $20 for the paperback

While the Collected was $14.35

Hyperbole, as I'd suspected

(Try and find Dave Smith's first book, Bull Island

For any price anywhere)

And I read some Jack Gilbert

And found his poems attractive enough

Though not, I felt, extraordinary

In a universe where much is

I considered one response:

Poetry isn't, of course, a competition

Some poems catch fire

Astonish and sometimes awe us

Reach into us like hands

And adjust

Sometimes remake us

O western wind, when wilt thou blow

Still some poems and some poets *are* better than others

So I tried out a second, waxed baroque:

Better than Shakepeare?

Than Frost, Yeats, Keats, Whitman, Dickinson, Hardy, Stevens,

       Auden, Moore, Lowell, Williams, Walcott?

Have you ever read Dante or Petrarch or Leopardi or Montale in
Italian?
Or Hugo or Baudelaire or Mallarme or Valery in French?
Or Milosz or Goethe or Jimenez or Aleixandre or Rilke, even in
translation?
I've read poetry every day for fifty or sixty years
And you, who have maybe read a thousandth
Are telling me what to read
Or I won't know what poetry is
And a third:
He's fine but I've seen better
I've *written* better poems than Jack Gilbert
Maybe that's what he wanted
Just a pleasant, old-fashioned shootout
Maybe he was just baiting me

6

But of course it wasn't really about poetry at all
Just a statement about terms
The terms of the relationship
He was willing to have with me now
With anyone
He was now a published author
An expert on wine
Paid to travel
He'd found a way to make money without working
And so felt he'd done better than I had
And wished to deprecate what I had become
While I didn't mind that in principle
Friends can overlook egotism and slights

But there is a responsibility to be who you are
To answer a challenge

It was not a conscious decision
But I can see now how I chose
I did not respond to his challenge directly
Instead I sent him
In a letter
A review of the wines we'd had
My wife and I
At a restaurant in the Bay area
A modest five-hundred-word essay
In his area of expertise
To answer his invasion of mine
I suggested he was free
To use or ignore what I'd sent
And I haven't heard from him since
I left him two more voicemail messages
And now it's been five years

That leaves me free to imagine
That he read my letter and sneered
This could never pass muster in my world
Too stiff, too cultured
Then later sold it to a Hungarian magazine
That published it in translation

7

Remuneration and regard are
In our capitalist society

Said to be
Felt to be
Earned
By risk taken
Effort, merit
Outcomes achieved

To appealingly share your opinion about wine
Reaps a greater return
Than teaching or nursing
Not value but profit governing
And so folks who by doing little
Do well
Often acquire inflated opinions
Of their opinions and skills
Or adopt such to cope with their guilt
Hollywood moguls
Wall Street brokers
Silicon Valley "entrepreneurs"
Crooners, sports stars
Wine critics

Our society sanctions their narcissism
And grants the steelworker, the miner, the primary care doctor
Lower status and less return
Prefers to those who labor
For the good of all mankind
Those who act in their own narrow interest
Perhaps they need it more than we do

Or, from a different vector
There are two primary images of the Jewish male

The greedy money lender
And the selfless committed scholar
One vengeful, driven, clannish
Touchy, hard to get to know
The other open and idealistic
Believing in justice, equality, mercy, and goodness
Indifferent to race, creed, and nationality
Friendship, to the former a means
Is to the latter a sacrament
Caricatures, certainly
But with some valid basis

8

Over the years I have lost many friends
Which must, it seems clear, reflect my failings
Made new ones to replace the old
It's true
But not a wash
The losses are more significant
Of those
Who could hold me to account
Knew who and what I once was
My value, promise, failings
Mirrors, microphones, signposts
Critics
Seeing them once in five years or ten
Was salutary
Whatever the posturing
Whatever the chagrin
And their praise meant more

Than that of the uninitiate
Brought tears

Nor can I blame this latest loss
On him
Despite my rhetoric
"You're so vain"
Not a fair appraisal
Perhaps I was still too great a threat
And he was simply happier
Not to have to conjure with me

Still it is, once again, checkmate
There is no way forward for us
Just another loss to accept
Like death and disability
Making me wish
We were better and smarter and stronger
That I was
A better man, a better friend, a better citizen
A better poet
That I could make us all see
How little time there is left
To get things right

Mockingbird Speaks

The mockingbird sweeps in, tail down

And lands on the fence

That and the cut grass

And the spongy ground underfoot

Revive an accumulation of old injuries and wrongs

Which our memory promptly stitches back to this version

The master life

Tattered but whole again

The bird starts to sing

You hear only the honey in my song

The liquid, heartbreaking beauty

Not the steely stridency

You see my fluid movement through the air

And do not feel the pain in both my wings

You see me free of nest, of food, of fate

As you would a fledged young girl free of family

Your prop, a natural phenomenon

My voice a supplement

To the perfume, the stream, the flowers

The sunlight, the hawk and hummingbird and grebe

But I have a precarious, individual life

I have put on hold to sing

As you might from a piano at a party

Every song I can recall

To forget the owl, the high wind

And the snow the air today augurs by nightfall

Intrepid

1

Because she trafficked outside my frame of reference
Chose South Africa fourth year when I chose England
Went alone while I brought a friend
Braved apartheid
(And I have still never been—probably never will be—close to the
southern hemisphere)
And spent a full year in high school alone in Japan
While I got as far as Wisconsin with my family
I accounted her intrepid
An explorer
And she never disappointed—
Until now

2

From England
I thought the *goal* was risk
Going as far and fast, seeing as much, as wild, as alien as possible
But see now she was just fitting in
Doing what seemed to her sensible
Fearless yes but not foolish
A different contract with, circuit breaker for, aspiration with regard to
Reality
She loved to learn is all
And was loved for that love in return

3

As consolation really for my mother
An introvert in my father's shadow
I invented an apothegm
"He's the dessert, but she's the main course"
It took within the family but was small comfort
Everyone loved my father
And that's how it was with Y.
Or perhaps a jot ampler
Because along with extroversion, and intrepidity
She was fortified by a conviction of rightness
Not the infuriating entitlement one demands or acquires
But the natural kind that comes of good fortune, of never being
                                        gainsaid

By chance merely, no fault of hers

4

She'd eased her way into life in Pasadena
Loved, comfortably off
Sheltered under the San Gabriel Mountains
Her landmarks: the Santa Anita Raceway, "the most beautiful track
                                      in the world"
Across the street from the LA County Arboretum;
The Pasadena Art Museum
(Today the Norton Simon; then "one of only three modern art
                                    museums in California")
The California Institute of Technology
"One of the world's top ten universities"
Home of the Jet Propulsion Lab, Murray Gelmann and Richard
                                    Feynman

The Huntington Library, Art Museum and Botanical Garden
The Rose Bowl, "the largest stadium in the country" with its
                                    annual New Year's Day parade
And who knows how many homemade ice creameries, world class
                                    goldsmiths, artists, inventors
Stravinsky at the Hollywood Bowl, Thomas Mann closing out his
                                    career in the neighborhood
Within reach of orange blossom, date and coconut palm, hummingbird
At the center, then, not like the rest of us
Not of some humble, admirable small American town
Nor of some materialistic industrial or commercial center
Crawling with lust for dominance
But of an American Athens
Garden, gallery, university, public forum
Striving for perfection
Halcyon before the smog, fires, mudslides
When water rights and immigration and politics were still clandestine

5

So no surprise then that *she* hosted *me*
On my first visit to Disneyland
Another backyard reach of her childhood legacy
She'd often been when young, but it had been years, she said
And she'd like to see what might have changed
Much had; none of it much mattered
We had become that unusual thing
Cross-sex friends
No pesky intimate interest in one another
Just her sunny appeal
(And whatever people then saw in me)

Going where the day took us
That day on one ride after another
A leisurely lunch
Medical school talk
And then, a loose ramble
About families, avocations

I recall, lulled by the sunlight
By the ease after steady application
By the pleasure of talking, for a change, without a censor
Telling her at Pirates of the Caribbean
Was there wine at lunch?
That I could have done it all better, Disneyland
(Certainly then it felt true
Seeing some splendid vision spread before me
Rainbowed, diamonded)
Which said more about her than me
How she elicited confidences
Encouraged daydreams, real ambitions

6

She fell in love twice, twice that I knew, while still at school
First with a straight arrow, then with a ne'er-do-well
Who was, agonizingly but mercifully, poached and discarded by
                                                 her roommate
So when she married
She by then far more practical
M. was more like the first than the second
Programmed in Silicon Valley

My wife, of course, liked her too
We never lost touch
Though, in those days, this was fairly typical:

A thousand apologies to both of you for my not answering your
                                        email and voicemail...
multiple reasons exist—away on vacation/looking at colleges,
M. away in China, my working as well as volunteering,
Familial disarray as M. was courted by two companies and found a
                                        new job—
but mostly the problem was not answering immediately,
before I got distracted by something else.
Does ADD appear with age or is it just getting worse??

7

We visited episodically, met M.
Once at their home in Monte Sereno
Once at an Indian restaurant in Santa Clara
Twice more we caught up with her alone where she docented
At the refurbished de Young
And again at the Palace of Fine Arts
She'd become a pediatrician
Had two children
Cultivated an ample garden
Was nurturer-in-chief
Depended upon, reliable
Bubbly still, an enthusiast
But now with a strong undertone of practicality

And then
Before the children had fully grown
M. was sent by Raytheon to Malaysia
And she and the children moved there with him for two years
She wrote a cultured, engrossing blog
We read every word
Envied her
Marveled again at how she managed to be that flexible
That open to experience that late in life

8

It is only by intuition, extrapolation, dead reckoning
That any of us can, even feebly, enter into another's distress
Learn what suffices to break her
How life brings even the intrepid to heel
Imposes age on youth
Eclipses confidence and resilience
And frightens or tortures or bludgeons us into submission
In her case, it seems, it was multiple sclerosis
Years of headaches and weakness
The threat of decline

In any case she's gone Dylan gentle
Chosen her own crystal cabinet
Bartered independence
For surrender to grave security
Once more she played hostess
Took us around the Carmel Valley facility
Expanding upon the two hundred residents
(One of them her mother at 96

Her father died there twenty years ago)
She presented it to us twirling, glowing
As she once presented Pasadena, Disneyland, Malaysia
The ultimate in comfort, safety, luxury

We ate in the dining room
Used pencils to circle our selections
On blue sheets of what looked like mimeographed paper
Reminiscent of worksheets from Junior High
The salmon patty, overcooked spinach, vanilla or chocolate ice
                                                cream
The grounds, the two rooms with sliding glass doors
Just a cheap condominium really
A half-step above the projects
Institutional food
And the promise of support
Should things deteriorate
Though only twelve percent of us ever require, ever enter a nursing
                                                home

The headaches are gone
And, with physical therapy
The weakness has subsided
The children are now on their own
Responsible now for her
Not she them
And we remain
Friends, sobered and chastened
For if she could become this, arrive here
What trip or trap or challenge, what certain ambush
Lies in wait for us, for you, just up ahead

Strokes

1

In the best marriages
Couples spend as much time together
As twins or lips or eyelids
Which augments their vulnerability
To injury or adversity of their partner's physical and emotional
person
Age, famine, war, disease, and random disaster threaten
Their fondest hope
That they from an optimal state until
Will suddenly, simultaneously depart

2

It was sunny
That day in Ogden
J. was out back when we arrived
Weeding high up in the newly terraced beds
They'd just carved
Out of the hillside
He was quieter
More self-contained than I remembered
S. affectionate and attentive
They took us for dinner
To a restaurant outdoors
He played down the dry eyes and diabetes
Highlighted his outdoor exploits
The skiing and hiking
His weight loss

3

Two secular New York Jewish mesomorphs
Both myopic with dark crimped hair, prediabetic
Cunning introverts, articulate, philosophical, independent
Successful physicians
Good fathers
(If the state of children at forty can be trusted)
Married well
Built robust lives
Moved them confidently around the country
For love, lifestyle, and money

4

I. was immersed in real estate
Took us to see their splashy Sarasota pied-a-terre
And the house on the sound
They'd lived in for two years
(And sold at a substantial profit)
A few doors down from Stephen King
But seemed more at home
By the touristy shore
Watching the people and pelicans passing
The sun dappling his smile
Exhilarated to have escaped Massachusetts
To have averted his destiny

Telling us about his nursing home patients
The income they represented
Never even hinting at their good fortune

In having his scrupulous, his judicious care
Before dinner
By the covered pool
And walking in their exclusive neighborhood
They were constantly at each other's throats
About continuing to pay the extortionate association fees
About keeping the Sarasota property
About the hurricane risk, the market
Where to go for dinner
But ritually, companionably
It was how they expressed
Both their independence and their love for each other

5

I have
Probably we all do
Wholly or partially
Compressed two people into one
From time to time
Movie stars
Laura Linney, say, and Leelee Sobieski
At one time Jeff Bridges, Dennis Quaid, and Kurt Russell
And there are the two Paul Guilfoyles (1902-61; 1949-still active)
Also acquaintances
From school or summer camp or work
Have cross-attributed credits, skills
Attitudes, gestures, faces
Overburdened one or the other with traits
Until
Disentangled

The resemblance submerged
Under floods, under seas of distinction

How we parse
Our short cuts
Associations and discriminations
Pattern recognitions
Placements, pigeonholes
Without enumeration
At barely a glance
Flicker of a smile, gait, voice
Catching not cataloguing
And, with luck
Fixing by a name
Anything but computing
Beautiful, mysterious
Astonishing
Sometimes falling short

6

"I just don't think most people
Recognize the importance of exercise," J. argued
"Or they aren't sufficiently motivated
I've been running to stay in shape
The diabetes is not going anywhere
So we go skiing every chance we get
Sundance, Park City, Big Basin
Places you won't have heard of
I no longer read philosophy like I did
Mostly politics now and history
Just finished *A History of Modern Germany*"

And he fell silent
Often would now
Looked past me out the window
I remembering, wondering what it was he saw

We shared a cadaver in Anatomy
Were designated drivers on group outings
To Napa, Sonoma, the Valley of the Moon
Again in class: assigned to draw one another's blood
He stuck me three times without success
And we were both approaching syncope
When a teacher intervened
I drew him without a wince
His blood glucose was 359
His first specific intimation of mortality

7

Of course they too were different
Perhaps most in their personae
J. serious, reliable, responsible
I. sloppy, lazy, demotic
Not fit to be invited to the same dinner party
Nor to work in the same department

J. majored in philosophy
Ran a psychiatry department
Became a downhill skier in his 40s
While I. claimed that he subscribed to the Annals of I.M.
As a knickknack for his son to mutilate

78

And yet I. wrote an article
About Alan Watts and medicine
The New England Journal of Medicine chose to publish
(For years I envied him that)
He was always a simplifier and minimizer
Humble in his way
Where J. augmented and amplified

Still both were attentive to
And considerate of
Their patients
They felt compelled to give different impressions
J. needed to be praised, felt worthy
I. needed not to

8

"You should have got out sooner
I eked out a small gain
Those penny stocks you told me about
You have to know when it's over"
I. let words out in discrete floods
As a lock does water
He would empty each burden first, then refill
It was off kilter and leisurely
"My son's up in New York now
Accountant
Largest firm in the state
And M.'s in law school
Might join A.'s firm when she graduates

This part of Florida's a great place to live
You really should move down"

He and I worked together ten years
Twenty-five clinic patients a day
Four nights of call a month
Covered four hospitals, 60,000 patients
Averaged four hours of sleep on call nights
It was intense
Sometimes we'd talk at lunch
Or visit between patients
There were fifteen of us at the Chicopee site

He and A. had dinner at our place
Once every three months for six years
With five other couples
A discussion group we called it
The impetus Ben Franklin's *Autobiography*
And we would each address a question posed in advance
Why are we here? and the like
They were outspoken, secure

9

It was their strokes
Left middle cerebral occlusions
That first alerted me to their similitude
Shared history, like inattention, can merge the disparate
Create new phyla
And so it was tragedy that drew my gaze
In particular loss of language

Cut off, dammed at its source
Loss of speech and the solace of reading
Not quite complete
But sufficient to taint all their enchantment
While still
Unlike the demented
Fully aware
And they were verbal people
In their lives and in their work

10

S. says, on the phone
As if we'd just been cut off mid-talk and reconnected
Taking up in mid-thought
Though it's been a couple of months
"Yes, J's decided to have the surgery
He's been triggering the cardioverter
A few times an hour
The risk is substantial
They say ten percent he may not come back from the procedure
But there doesn't seem to be much choice...

"I keep busy
I still get to my reading groups
But it's difficult
J.'s despondent and uncommunicative
He wants me around all the time in case

"We listen to music and dinners are nice
He watches a lot of television

And he sits in the chair and stares
At the floor, the walls, out the window
It's hard for *him*
I don't know what goes on in his head anymore
Know as little as I do now about my daughter in New York
Or my new neighbor, who I hardly get to see"

When we first met, S. worked at the zoo
Fed and cared for animals
Cleaned their cages
Later she managed travel for physician practices
She's tall, taller than J.
Has a frank open face
Radiates something classical
Poise, calm, competence, loyalty
Never fussed, sometimes bustled
Went for the jugular when appropriate
But stylishly, intuitively
Made home a haven
For J., for his friends

11

If language distinguishes us from the animals
Then its loss is a kind of death
Or at least demotion
What connects us to one another
Community, history, commerce, love, argument, precision
Gone in a flash
Conversation, one-sided, flags
Despite encouragement from eyes, grunts, nods, familiar features

* *

Halting, remembering
Wondering what they remember
Feeling the cold vacuum
Of the gap between minds
Do we really know what another
Any other
Perceives, feels, thinks
Why, even how, he does what he does
Even when he can tell us

12

"We're doing fine
Went up to D.C. for a few days
Visited relatives, friends
Enjoyed the change
We've been thinking of coming to visit you
Our son's doing well
Found a house in Westchester
Still with the same large firm
And M.'s planning to take over the practice
Over the next year or two
I'm getting older
I wouldn't mind more time at home
But she still has a lot to learn
So maybe a year from now"

A.'s Armenian
Very attached to her family
Grew up in Thailand
Runs a law practice

Has for decades
Is, like I., a minimizer
Cites travel
As if a stroke were inconsequential
Radiates competence, confidence and warmth
All qualified
Recantable if not justified by any particular beneficiary
Fancies large, well-appointed dwellings
Insists on them, politely but firmly
Expresses herself bluntly and with feeling
Republican, unfazed
Loyal, certain
On casual terms with fate

13

"Fat, female, and forty—cholecystitis"
They taught us in medical school;
Later, I discovered fat, female and fifty—subarachnoid hemorrhage
And fat, male and sixties—ischemic stroke
Statistical mnemonic aides for diagnosis
AKA lumping, as Darwin put it
Yet, as Tolstoy has it
"All happy families are like one another
And each unhappy family
Is unhappy in its own way"
Splitting
And each stroke is different from every other
And what constitutes happy
When fifty percent of marriages end in divorce
And the reasons for staying married are so diverse

We all belong to a myriad of families
More than we can grasp or fathom
More than we ever come to know
And we all belong to them in different ways
And for different reasons
Families of risk
Families of triumph
Families of loss
Every day we learn about who and what we are
And every day the lumps and splits multiply
Some trivial, others defining
A squint, a scar, a drawl, a lopsided grin
A stroke, a spouse

14

And we all want each him back
Them back together
As they were
It undone
Because the waste
Is, as death is
Unfair, premature
But more so because it should be reversible
Retrievable, replaceable
We want no story
No poem
Things back as they were
Tenuous, contingent
As threatening as promising
But sovereign individuals back in charge

Everything possible
If unlikely
Not final
Not done

15

The best lives oscillate between intercourse and action
And silence and contemplation
Which leaves most humble, daunted
All this clamor about living
The relative health, happiness or misery
A few years more or less
Of a few privileged creatures
All to be dead and forgotten
In ten or twenty or at the most thirty years
Held together here for a moment
By this mendacious poem
A devious snapshot of one mind
Trying to enlist disparate lives
Into a forced and fleeting harmony
The way a kaleidoscope tumbling
Can for a moment draw beauty from chaos by chance

But beauty and coherence are in the eye of the beholder
That eye, its mind, that may be gone tomorrow
At one stroke will be gone sooner or later
And all that will remain
A short while longer
These feeble characters
Strokes upon a page

And whatever bare remnant of the fellowship
The love we all felt for one another
That they convey

III. Unassuming Mastery

"the achieve of, the mastery of the thing!"

> Gerard Manley Hopkins,
> "The Windhover"

"...experience, acquired in humility and with hard work, means everything."

> Patrick Süskind, *Perfume: the Story of a Murderer*

A Daurian Rhododendron Comes Out

It was another cold, long, leafless winter, my fifth
Each previous spring I've been threadbare
Patchy with youth

Now suddenly
Without warning
I'm glorious

Covered circumferentially
Covered root to crown
In blossom

A truer purple than aubergine
And more delicate than lilac
Lacy, provocative, smart

So many have come to call
Honey bee, bumble bee, and fly
A thrush, a wren, even a goldfinch

Yet even should the weather hold
No storm, no violent winds
It will only last a week or two

After that it will be another year
Of unobtrusive leaves and mossy branches
Unnoticed except by spiders in my corner of the yard

Shrinking and filmy
With small translucent flowers

* *

I find myself embarrassed by my brassy kin
Embarrassed too by the showy irises, camellias, and magnolias
Impressed only with the earlier blooming daurian rhodo
I admired, partial view, through the gate, the other side of the wall

As it flowered, as I have since
As if in imitation
A full month on

An homage
A simulacrum
Love, I suppose, in a humble way

Anatomy of an Improbable Friendship

1

Though we have tried
(And generally failed)
To revive friendships
We have never tried to build one
They have all grown
Organically
Sprung up like mushrooms or weeds
Without plan or guidance
Then seem, once they sprout, to depend for survival
Only on shared enthusiasm
Or failing that
Willingness to maintain them
Which does, with time, often seem to flag
Why and how they first prosper
Remains to us a provocative mystery

2

By that time, 1977, intern in Boston June 30
Resident in Honolulu July 1
The program I joined
Was termed integrated
Rotation through five primary training hospitals
Queen's—academic; Kaiser—prepaid HMO
St. Francis—poor folk; Straub—rich folk
Kuakini—middle class Japanese folk
University of Hawaii Integrated Medical Residency Program

Each site with a program director
Three male, two female
All readily accessible
A vital component of our tuition

3

N.B. had preceded integration
Started to serve St. Francis, ground up, 1970
Its program director by 1977
We residents were free to trade months
A St. Francis for a Kaiser
A Queen's for a Straub
I traded away one Straub
One Kaiser and both St. Francis
So spent only one elective month there
Renal, call every other night
Never came up for air
Barely knew N.B. as manager
But we chatted on social occasions
And found much common ground

4

She too was integrated
The many divisions of her interest
The many strands of her genealogy
Her ideas about medical management
The inclusivity of her considerations, methods, and friendships

Her eclectic high and low tastes
Drawn into a stable, flexible
Tranquil, reassuring unity
So that she suited her position
Took an active and responsible interest
In everything and everyone under her purview
And in the world around her

5

Simply being on Oahu
We shared plumeria, orchid, and bougainvillea
Coral reefs and black sand beaches
Brief light afternoon "pineapple" rains
Short mail runs to neighboring
Kauai, Maui, and Molokai
Kukui, hibiscus, bird of paradise
Nene, amakihi, akepa
Lingering sunsets over the ocean
The Likelike Highway to Kaneohe and Kailua
The Pali Lookout, Diamond Head, Pearl Harbor
Pastel balconied four story buildings
Haleiwa and the North Shore
Hanauma Bay and the Blow Holes
Makapuu Beach and body surfing
Voices echoing in salt-softened air
Haiku Gardens and the Byodo-In Temple
Haoles together
On contiguous parts of the island

6

The program was no frills practical
Ideal for hands-on experience
In the guts and jolts of everyday patient care
Preparation sensible and efficient
No pretention, theory, or disguise
Kuakini the most pragmatic
And least supervised
Was the one I traded for
Its attraction enhanced by the ICU/CCU nurse
I met over the heart monitors
Who has been my wife now for forty-two years
But valued for the scathing
Of rapid turnover
Long days
Demanding call
Multiple taxing variations on common problems

7

N.B. also had a foursquare no frills practical side
Evident in the first letter she sent us
"Paradise stinks. UPW#1 union has been on strike five weeks
Which means no garbage collection.
Also no laundry, cooking or janitorial services
At the public schools, state hospitals, prison"
She took to Anita as readily as to me
Had her Hans, whom we met briefly at functions
Promised fair to one day replace Irv Schatz
As Program Director

At home there after ten years
If still ambivalent

8

But was too an optimist and explorer
Modest and energetic
Which might begin to explain
"Your letter was a breath of fresh air
Thanks for thinking of me
I'm happy your career is off to a great start
I envy your status as super internist
You and I well know general internists
Are treated as second-class citizens in Honolulu"
And "This fall I finally made my first trip to Europe
I traced my roots
By visiting all the historical sites
Of King Robert the Bruce of Scotland
I am his direct descendant
I bought a bagpipe
And am driving Hans crazy
With my practicing"

9

Still without ACP meetings, it might have ended there
The American College, the best source
Of internal medicine physician continuing education
Met in New Orleans, April 1980
Our first time there

And she introduced us to Bourbon Street
To Jackson Square, the Garden District
Brennan's, Galatoire's, Antoine's
Café du Monde, Broussard's, and Court of Two Sisters
Went out to dinner with us one evening
That became, for us, an ACP tradition
Each year, as the demand for her time grew
She reserved one night for dinner with us
(Hans, an oceanographer
Had his own voyages
As far as we ever knew
They rarely traveled together
Certainly not to the ACP)

10

The greater her reputation grew
The less she liked to talk shop
Was more interested in Anita's shopping
Than my innovations at work
When the ACP met in DC
We went together to Monticello
From Philly to Longwood Gardens
Between 1980 and 1994
Between dinners
Anita and I moved from IA to MA to CT to IL
(Small HMO, large HMO, Yale, U of IL & the VA)
While N. consolidated her position at St. Francis
And moved up in the ranks of the ACP
But when Dr. Schatz left
The cunning, autocratic Queens-based cabal

Took control
While Hans was having a midlife crisis
All just in time for the 1994 ACP
"My life is in major transition right now
Will I have stories to tell you in Miami!"

11

That was bravado
The N. we'd known was always upbeat, always the optimist
But had been rejected twice that year
At work and at home
Was poised to move to Cleveland
And was hurt and angry and struggling
To understand what had happened
And put it behind her
Stories to tell indeed
Spent most of *that* conference together
Attended the same sessions
Drove to the various places she wanted to visit
Empathized, sympathized, listened
We'd had this time and again
Rejection, relocation
But felt we probably deserved it
And we had each other
She'd been so solid, so reliable
That the threat felt like a war or a hurricane
A rank injustice
Knew too, she was strong
Would prevail; did

12

Were by then clearly friends
Spent a weekend with her in Cleveland
And when the Cleveland job, which started well
Self-destructed after five years
And she transferred to a better one
In Youngstown
Knowing what moves are like
Drove the nine hours from Champaign
To help her settle
Unpack, organize, move furniture
Limo'd her cats
Shadow and Midnight from Cleveland
To their new home
Went together to the Niagara-on-the-Lake Shaw Festival
Silk shop, tea at Prince of Wales, craft fair
Fanny's First Play, Six Characters in Search...
The Millionairess, Laura
Wineries, sculpture studio, fruit stands
Just before we moved again, this time west

13

Once in Fresno
We were again reduced to ACP meetings
And after my retirement
To annual letters and phone calls
So in January 2018
We proposed an Alaskan cruise
At first enthusiastic

She in the end decided
"I do not think this is a trip I would enjoy
Despite the lovely company
The early rising hours
And frequent on-ship/off-ship
Is just not right for me
I think the best way
To rendezvous
Is for me to fly on up to visit
Probably in 2019"

14

"Please do visit next year," we replied
"We have a lovely room waiting for you
With all the privacy the cruise did not promise"
But she didn't, probably couldn't
And she died in 2020
Our friendship still an improbable serendipitous mystery
(Also now irretrievable and irreplaceable)
I keep wanting to show her, ask her
Did I do us justice
Did I get it right
The fifth of our friends
To have died in the past five months

# Backbone

1

When its first pink flowers begin to open in January
Most of the other plants do not even have leaves
Then crocus, daffodil, daphne, and windflower
Cherry, lilac, and apple petals come and go
One tree after another leafs out
Azalea, iris, even early rose arise
And the scentless camellia seems still to have the vigor of youth
As unassuming and enthusiastic, as comfortable in any company
As it was at the start all alone
It is only the fragrant pieris that has shared its lifespan
But in another inaccessible region of the yard

2

She wrote "This year has been a settled-in-and-enjoying-it year
                                              for me...
Most outsiders still regard Cleveland as 'the Mistake by the lake'
But it is truly a renaissance city... In honor of Cleveland's two
                                              hundredth birthday
I wish to share with you my adopted city...
So in no particular order, these are my fifteen favorite Cleveland
                                              things:

...

2. The Holden Arboretum—2,900 acres with twenty miles of paths
The largest arboretum in the US; it's a wonderful place to ride my
                                              horse

...

4. Playhouse Square—four old vaudeville theaters were renovated
Beginning in the late '70s to provide six acres and 7,000 seats for
                                        live theater and ballet
This is the largest theater restoration in the world.
...
6. The Cleveland Indians—No World Series win yet, but just wait—
..."
And later: "I am grateful for good friends, good family
And a sustaining sense of adventure for whatever life sends my way"
Curiosity, enthusiasm, optimism and energy
Radiate from each page she wrote
Though she could not know then it would end so soon
It was only her second of four years in Cleveland

3

Some, as we did, find such energy attractive
Some find its relentlessness forced, false, and irritating
And some see it as a resource to exploit

4

Cleveland came at the end of a long, stable, quiet, positive decade
All her communications had been terse
And limited to family, travel, and progress at work
She and "her Hans" were by then a power couple
But one more interested in service than self
He'd become Chairman of the U of Hawaii Ocean Engineering
                                        Department
She'd made presentations and written papers

Been promoted to U of H Deputy Program Director, then Program
                                                        Director
Been elected ACP Governor for the Hawaii Chapter, then ACP Regent
Been designated an ACP master practitioner
(Twenty of us are every year out of 200,000)
Hans went on research trips and she to her ACP meetings
And in 1987 "It was an auspicious year for Hans
He found his father, taken by the Nazis in Poland
And presumed dead all these years
In May we went to Ludwigsberg, W. Germany to meet him
He is 78 and in great health. It was a wonderful reunion"
They even took up ocean kayaking

5

Not everyone is inspired by origins
Her first two trips to Europe were to visit
First her father's roots in England, Scotland, and Scandinavia
And then her mother's in Transylvania
("Maternal grandparents still alert and healthy in their 80s
Were from villages in Hungary
That are now part of Romania")
She met cousins there
Of whom even her grandparents were not aware
And she returned to both Scotland and Hungary time and again

During that decade they seemed to move
From strength to strength
From joy to joy
Events abetting their optimism and energy
And expanding their reach

6

Still, no one escapes trauma
Her father died the year after she visited his Scotland roots
And her sister died of a brain cancer three years later
(She took six months off to be with her towards the end)
And she, godmother to her then six-year-old daughter
A responsibility that grew to guardian when her father, soon after,
also died
And to encompass economic as well as emotional support
She herself fell from a horse at full gallop in Hungary
Had "right brain damage"
"Considerable memory loss"
And was "surviving the emotional impact of having to accept
A 'new' me"
Still for a long time their trajectory was onward, upward, outward

7

Though beauty is in the eye of the beholder
And there is no accounting for taste
There are beauty pageants and lists of mosts
And jokes and consensuses (consenses? consensi?)
Which suggest that taste is in any case not entirely random
But inhabits a continuum from bellezza through normalezza to
brutezza
With gradations of cute, pretty, elegant, gamine, and the like
To broaden the range of attractiveness
Even plain and mannish
Being preferable, at least linguistically, to ugly

8

After fifteen years of partnership and fifteen years of consistent
                                        employment
Starting over is, if not traumatic, at least stressful
And to move alone to do it
From Hawaii to Cleveland
Where you know, well, no one
It's fortunate that she had the ACP network
And her reputation to soften the landing
Since the Cleveland Clinic
Formidable history notwithstanding
Was no help at all
"My hospital just sold itself to a for-profit company
Not by choice but because of the enormous debt it has accumulated
Over time by its commitment to care for the indigent...
The one thing that keeps me going
(Besides the need to pay my mortgage!)
Is my commitment to the residents...
Don't be too surprised, however, if, in a few years
I ... go full time into long term care
I already am part-time medical director for a local nursing home"

9

Two years later the Cleveland Clinic was bankrupt
But by then she had cut her losses and moved to Youngstown
Her eighty-hour work week down, temporarily, to fifty
Though never one to be idle

She'd prior to that also graduated from
The Physician's Executive Institute
Of the Case Western Reserve University
Weatherhead School of Business Management
Become a geriatric subspecialist
And graduated the Shaker Heights Citizen's Police Academy
"Courses included crime scene investigations, subduing of suspects…
Hostage negotiations… jail management… police patrol ride-alongs"
Was doing police work in her "free" time
And contriving still to manage that nursing home in Cleveland

10

Each of us is always changing
But when we envision the people we've known
We generally telescope their various selves
Into some congenial epoch
With N.B., for us, it was Cleveland/Youngstown when, as she put it
"I try to be as decadent as possible
For me this is limited to my usual eccentric behavior"
Her horse, Frankie Dustin
Her cats, Midnight and Shadow
Her collections of everything from netsuke
Through oriental furniture and foo dogs
To garden gnomes, keepers and fairies
Her baby grand classical piano ("Liszt is my favorite"), bagpipes,
                                                        fiddling
And "even built a mountain dulcimer with lots of help" in West
                                                        Virginia
(After her third move in six years, she wrote
"With all the STUFF I have accumulated, I estimate it will take

107

At least thirty years to empty all the boxes. So it becomes a contest
Which will come first, death or completion of unpacking"
It was the latter; though the former came too soon)
Her childlike love of shopping, bananas foster, and steak tartare
Her two or more substantial trips each year
Regular "intellectual retreats" to Chautauqua
And theater "glut" at Stratford Shakespeare and Niagara-on-the-
                                        Lake Shaw Fests
Three weeks in China/Tibet/Nepal, another three in Australia/New
                                        Zealand
Germany and Spain by car for five weeks
African safari, three-day stay in a lighthouse on the Maine Coast
Budapest and Krakow both before (1981) and after (2011) the Iron
                                        Curtain fell
Inline skating, ziplining, hiking, white water rafting
("I love to try new things and to take justifiable risks")
Anchorage and Kenai
Costa Rica and Iceland—both twice in succession
And once she'd cut back at work, needlepoint, cross stitch
Sketching, watercolor, acrylics
And plans to write Haiku, short stories, and a novel

11

In March of 2005 she wrote:
"So far... a tough year
Nothing unmanageable, just stressful
At work... a bipolar resident
Trying to save his life and career
Then this week a first year resident
Collapsed while on call

Found to have superior vena cava syndrome
From a tumor in that vessel
He's in the ICU

On the home front a close friend
(A nurse I've known since medical school
Who lived in the Akron area)
Died last January age 64
Had pulmonary hypertension
And a tough last few months
Hospitalized three weeks at the Cleveland Clinic in December
Then January in a nursing home for deconditioning rehab
Had no family
Gave me power of attorney for health care
Called one morning at work by the nursing staff
End of January
They had found my friend comatose
Cardiac arrest followed
She could not be resuscitated
Two other friends and I were left to arrange
Funeral, burial, find a probate lawyer (no will)
And clean out her apartment
What a mess, and very sad"

12

So, N., we'll dispatch one last letter of our own
It's been a warm spring
But just now we are having some much needed rain
Last week we had our first guests (outdoors) in fourteen months
One, an exemplary physician in his forties
On leave due to stage four colon cancer
And now, since there's no more risk of embarrassment

We're free to broadcast our gratitude
Of course, for your friendship
But more that you *did* stay young
Were a universal friend
Construed your obligations generously
Caretaker, godmother, guardian, executor, governor, regent, friend
One of the six hundred program directors nationwide
Who trained two new generations of primary care and hospital
                                                    internists
Improved the quality of that training
Worked seventy- and eighty-hour weeks
Neither workaholic nor saint
Just an integral pedicle in the backbone of our nation
Why, in the face of greed and corruption
Things still work here

So, as you instructed
No memorial service, no obituary
Just an appreciation
A cross-stitch to reveal how a life can be lived
Honorably, honestly, enjoyably, usefully
The way the camellia lives
And leave us, though sorrowful, smiling

An Insect Aside

The fly
On all fours
Has a dog's thorax
But such flexible wires for arms
Wires she rubs together
As if paring them
For flight
She moves with the clamor and decisiveness
Of youth
Barreling through summer
Flailing demoniacally around everything that stirs

The yellow jacket moves with the poise of a greater age
Insinuating her deep amber into the very meshes of autumn
Brushing aside the sand on the cement with her restrained flight
Hanging about the aging blackberries and currants
Walking upon those fine hairy legs
The quiet confidence of slow flight
And the low hum of contentment
Resonate among the turning leaves
As a cello among violins
Another dangerous voice
In a membrane no larger than a berry
Perhaps the very seed of winter
Striped and still and chanting

College Friend

1

We stood composed
On one of the round marble tables
In NoYes lounge
Designed for Vassar College
By the Eero Saarinen
Of St. Louis arch fame
Surrounded by a sea
Of dormitory mates
On Naugahyde couches
In hot pink, purple, orange, blue
Impulsively invited to witness
Our amateur enactment
Of *Waiting for Godot*

No, we had no formal theatrical training
But had spent months
In each the other's company
Avid students of Firesign Theatre
And one another
Had learned timing, gestures
Sense of humor, dislikes
Better than the chemistry
And economics
We took in regulation classrooms
With credentialed teachers
Before naturally progressing to Beckett

I cannot weigh the quality
Of our performance

Though our audience
Free of our private preoccupations
Was silent, open-mouthed, attentive
And effusive after
Of course we were not really acting
Just in thrall to an intense concentration
Which soon after spilled over
From the Beckett to other texts
And into the wider world
Of women, movies, politics
Music, travel
A whole life could come of what we shared

2

Chorus

He was that year a man standing
To one side of himself
A pendulum can only reach
Maximum displacement
Has no annex, no attic
No mirror world
When grade school restraint yielded
To college freedom
The sixties
And his anarchic friend
Drove him
Far beyond any continuum
And he found himself
Also beyond harmonics
No rebound possible

And settled there
For the time satisfied
And only returned
Quite unintentionally
The long way round

3

We were besotted one afternoon
With Paul McCartney
Wings' *Wild Life*
Imprinting on "Some People Never Know"
Other hours, other days
We played Frisbee
In the park
Paid minute ritual attention
To each little thing that caught our fancy
The pinball machine in the basement
Pizza and Dirty Muthas on College Avenue
Dated roommates
Took them to New York City
A free preview of *Gimme Shelter*
Ran in morning sunlight
Around the tranquil lake
Saw, in New Paltz
The Graduate, Butch Cassidy
Midnight Cowboy
Open, free and undetermined
Taking whatever came

Once with two avid friends
We signed on for a late summer canoe trip

Far up into Canada
Drove from New Jersey
Fifteen hours north
Pushed off late in the day
In a blinding rain
Against the wind
And before we'd debarked
Had had enough
Tented, cold dinnered, slept
And retraced our vanished wake
Again against a pivoted wind
And hitchhiked home

Another rainy night
This one under the picnic table
Of a burger joint
A morning in Plattsburgh
One car an hour entering the Thruway

Persisting
We did get back
Didn't perhaps know our own minds yet
Craved dead ends, labyrinths, runarounds
Achieved less than we grew
Did it together
Friends, I thought, for life

4

Chorus

He had a droll sense of paradox
Could halt the flow of time

Bring the cosmos to a standstill
And see it clear
If bewildering
Was lonely as a child
Couldn't tally
Wanted to, desperately
Mimicked his less thoughtful
More popular, anarchic
Older brother
Slackened his grasp
To please his peers
Found a self
That, at equilibrium
Was healthy, viable and attractive
But never satisfied
Worked
But did not fit
Later shucked it
Like a shell or skin

5

Changed majors four times
Ending in economics
Drawn to Eugen Loebl
Beacon of virtue and resistance
Joined an idealistic inner circle
Of philosophical economists
A discipline that didn't/doesn't really exist
Imbibing a unique socialism
From a committed Communist

On our distaff American college campus
Was student rep
On the Development Board
For the townhouses
The school's first non-dormitory housing
Had three or four
Multifaceted, self-contained
Ambitious girlfriends
Lovely, gracious

One moved to a townhouse with us
When they opened senior year
Coeducational, cutting edge
Across the street from campus
We made schedules
Shopped, cooked, cleaned, fought
Planted bulbs, washed windows
Made budgets, fell out
Made up
Finished our course work
Our finals/dissertations
And scattered

6

Chorus

Eugen Loebl was a Czech hero
But a minor one
Czech government in exile, 1944
Victim of Slansky purge trial, 1952
(Sentenced to life in prison
Rehabilitated)

Finance minister for Dubcek, 1968
Exiled by the Russian invasion, same
Teacher at Vassar, 1970
An actor played him
In Costa-Gavras' *The Confession*
But was onscreen less than a minute
And Costa-Gavras is known for Z
And *State of Siege*
Not *The Confession*

To students at Vassar College
He was a European giant
To Czechs a worthy bit player
He confused both alike
With his insights, integrity
And impractical wisdom

7

He got to California before me
Once arrived
I'd visit him often in the informal commune
Where he boarded the first few years
(We'd often wait in Noe Valley
Around the block
For Bud's ice cream)
Before he bought a fixer-upper
And fixed it up
New floors, new roof
Sheetrock, paint, windows
Doorknobs, plants

Cabinets, counters
Built a desk from raw lumber
Lived in the midst of it all
For the experience
And the profit
By then he seemed
Like Jackson Pollock, Jeff Kern
If they were/are who *they* seemed
Working class, handy, independent
Ingenious, methodical

Until he landed a job
With Bank of America
He would say
When asked what he did
"Projects"
First he joined them
Then ran them
His Walt Whitman-like brother
Who
After a stint in the military
Another, longer, as a hippie
In Mendocino
Owned and operated
A successful coffee house
In San Francisco
Would belly laugh
Joyously/gleefully
Ask him, "What does that mean
Projects
What kind of work is that?
People live in projects

When they can't afford better
That's not work"
And a new Mike would smile in deprecation
Nod his head
And equivocate

8

Chorus

Perhaps things were frightening
Perhaps just hard
Perhaps there was too much contradiction
Or at least no resonant affirmation
As he rebuilt his house
Standing, a colossus
On his own choices & skills
Seeing deep
Into the foundation of things
And then left for work
Where he was managed
Channeled
Precious and specialized
Perhaps he did not want to fight anymore
Against convention, stupidity, license
Probably it was just loneliness
No longer feeling like he owned his self

9

In time he married
The woman seemed an odd choice

120

After the fashionable girls he'd known
Dowdy, dogmatic, demanding
And down to earth
No sense of humor
No interest in the arts
Little in clothing
His mother had been an Edith Bunker
His father a Willy Loman
But the wife he chose
Had sharper edges
And not an ounce of sensitivity
Or eccentricity
Practical, materialistic, and immovable
As the moraine glaciers leave behind

And then came their trip to London
"Never again," he told me
"I didn't know what to do with myself
For ten days
Museums, sites, concerts
Really what's the point?
From now on, I will travel
Only when I have something to do
For work
A negotiation, a course
Never without a practical purpose"
Once we'd talked daily
Now less than once a year
So I couldn't see the stages
Just the transformation

By the next time we met
There was nothing/no one left

She had eaten him to a husk
As ants do a grasshopper
He looked at her before he spoke
Held conventional media views
I don't blame her
It was what she was made to do
But he chose her
Took her for better
Or worse
Stayed

10

Chorus

There is a narrative
False but gripping
Each, it says, can return
To any prior unstable state
We grow organically
Nature nurtured
In a smooth untroubled reversible way

In fact, though
Anything but
All growth is saltatory
Violent, uneven, random, fierce
And irrevocable
There is no understanding it
And no going back
One second harmony
The next discord

There is never more peril
Than when the sun shines
And the world is halcyon

He had vigorously examined his life
Then (gradually? suddenly?) stopped
Was two men
Incompatible
Was the later a pre-fixed personality
A naturalistic had-to-happen
Built to his father's prototype?
Was the former only a distortion
Inspired by youth, time, place, and friends?
Just a larva
Waiting
Might he/could he have become
What he so richly promised?
What was he/is he/are we?
Compounded of what? How free?

11

To me it doesn't matter anymore
What he chose and became
What he was
Shines in my memory
The tight curls of his wiry hair
His eyes, liquid brown
His mischievous smile
Weighing a sally
Sharing a past foolishness

Fit, light, high-waisted
Undismayed
Looking out the dorm window
At the trees in the distance
Critical, confident, assertive

I have time and again
Started over, met new people
Made new friends
Always with friends
There are the two
Simultaneous perspectives
How you are together
And how the friend appears
He was
Which is why I miss him
A paragon
A prototype of both

Early Tulips

She said, as I sat in the chair
And she cut my hair: *I wish*
The weather would settle
My tulips are starting to blossom
They don't know what's coming
And I can't tell them
But the radio says there'll be a storm, ice and cold
So it isn't going to end well
Suddenly it all came back so vividly:

That New Year's Eve
Was it 1962? 3? 4?
He was still so promising, so viable
I could see a statesman, a writer
Fame, accomplishment
He spoke with confidence
Knew his own mind
And his place in the world

So, I am confident
The conventional wisdom is wrong
It was not inevitable
Given parents, brother
Financial troubles
That he would lose his way

No, he didn't suffer
He committed failure
He could not tolerate loneliness
His own eccentricity

So shut the door on his future
In his early teens

You will probably, understandably, say
Joining the Key Club
Made perfect extracurricular sense
Helped to build his college resume
Service and fellowship
Are laudable goals
How could that do him harm?

You didn't know him then
What joining meant to him
Key Club was no part of his earlier aspirations
Hopes or heritage
Having no aptitude for sports
It was, for him, the closest thing
In high school to a fraternity

He wanted to be hazed and accepted
To hide; and was willing, eager
To surrender who he was
That was my first of many
Lifetime Cassandra moments
I had seen others go off the rails
But this time I lived, knew, and shared
The promise, pain, fear, and weakness
And said what I knew as warning
I might have been trying
To convince a fish to fly

* *

It has all ended as I knew then it would
He never recovered
Had trouble in his work
With his relationships
In his public and private life
He has been erratic, inept, and miserable
There has been no redemption

But what could I say
Even now, knowing what I know
What could anyone say
To that promising young man
Around the time of his Bar Mitzvah
How address the mystery
What is it makes character?
Determines readiness?
Delivers or divides men from their happiness?

Exploit

The dragon in the basement coughs and roars
He is an ancient beast
Legend has it his back was broken in battle
That since then his fire stays in his belly
And he cannot eat solid food
He sleeps now and forgets through the long languor of summer
Until cold wakens him to new pain
And he roars his anguished roar
Aged, his wings and legs are palsied, helpless
He has not seen his children in a thousand years
All, he suspects, are by now as he is, captives or worse
His hoard reduced to an engrammatic tintype buried in his skull
Staying upright, sleepless all winter, grows harder each year
He remembers the sunlight on fresh snow
The wind under his wings
The river running its steel knife through the land
And then the flowers bleeding from the ground
Recalls his freedom in his harnessed pain
His roar shakes the house
And we are warmed

Truncated

1

Sideswiped
In his descent of October
By a lethal diagnosis
He skidded off the calendar
And beyond the deceit of words

Continued upright
But mostly in the middle of the night
Could no longer laugh
Knowing it's likely cut his life
In half

He's resolved
To seek repair
While soldiering on
Into the dark and frigid air
Into twilight

2

Behind him a sacrosanct childhood
(Like ours)
Its indelible set of images
Awash with sentiment
The grammar school construction
Of the hull
Junior high affixing of the deck

The high school masts and spars
College sails
Medical school anchor and rudder

(And all along the byways, travels, and entanglements
An afternoon alone in the dusty basement
Of a bookstore with old magazines
Adrift in a previous century
A week's cruise in the gaudy rich Caribbean
Two love triangles
Marriage
A transfer two thousand miles west)

Then as house officer
The proctored early ventures in the harbor
And finally sails up
Some first independent maneuvers
On the high seas of practice

Finding his sea legs
Capable and ambitious
He specialized
Outfitted his vessel
First for fishing
Then for battle

And suddenly formidable
Ordered to sweep a Central American harbor free of mines
He starts south
And into a freak storm

Lightning sets fire to the mainmast
Forty foot waves
Sweep away forecastle
And rudder...

3

Of course, it's not a boat
It's a life
And it's not over
That's the problem with poetry
It ennobles, distances, and tragicizes
What's short, nasty, intimate, bleak, and unpredictable
(My muse proposed sedate here:
Late autumn landscape, dusk, and covert rhyme)
Enables the intolerable
Or, in another key, whines
All the instruments agree
It never gets the tone quite right
Asks us to join it on Helicon
When what's needed is stillness, silence, and time

4

Sorry
This is the end of the broadcast day

Appendix

1

I'd call him innocent
If anyone could have still been that
In his twenties
Late in the twentieth century

Or naïve, ingenuous
But then you'd likely (mistakenly) blame him
And if I say unsophisticated
I will have to qualify

Only about relationships
He was a cultivated scientist
Accomplished outdoorsman
Subtle in argument and understanding

And neither nerd nor geek
Not grungy or subversive
Attractive, shy and likeable
And if not popular, accepted

So unsophisticated then
With qualifications as noted
And no pejorative intent
About love relationships in particular

2

If you were to need general surgery
Appendix or gallbladder
Hernia, colon polyp
He's the guy you'd want

Starting in the first month of the first year
He spent most night fifteen miles away at SMC
Assisting at surgeries
And annotating textbooks

While the rest of us med students
Were drinking beer, studying
Watching movies, reading novels
Then sleeping

His father was a surgeon
He knew from the first he would be too
And he did vascular as well
Tranquilly assuming the extra responsibility and hours

3

Though he was a more than modest introvert
He made a good, not first perhaps
But down-the-road impression
On colleagues and coworkers

Was chosen as friend or something more
Taken in fact in med school

133

By Jane, another student, for two years
As roommate and lover

But felt himself entering a darkness, defenseless
That he might still end up alone
Or obliged to compromise
To live a multiple choice life

He had not grown or learned to choose himself
Needed to
Wanted, needed to learn
And (sort of) did

4

In nearly every life, one choice
That of a life partner
Is fraught, iterative, intractable
And irrevocable, definitive

For him it, somehow
When it finally came, came easy
It may have been the purity, the innocence (there, I got to say it)
Of his gaze and heart

That drew the same from others
Or his exquisite sensitivity
Beginner's
Or blind luck
But he used the skill
He'd sort of learned

Just the once, his choice so faultless
The knack became irrelevant

5

She clearly knew what he was
Instinctively respected and protected him
Surrounded him with warmth
And affection

Extended his family
Beyond his imagining
So naturally that
It all seemed preordained

But he never came to underestimate
The value of the opportunity he'd had to choose
That brief open season, open sesame
Which had set his life on its true trajectory

6

Four children, a wealth of friends
Working together at the hospital
Hiking and biking
In the mountains and backcountry; to work

A full life, intimacy, happiness
That is what he sees, looking back

* *

This time we don't have to choose just one right word
They all apply
It does make one wonder
How they're related
Style and content of courting
And happy marriages

Are vestigial rudiments, is a stump, enough
Not alpha male, just a basic alphabet
Is it the thought that counts?
Can a nonverbal meat heart be eloquent?

He has never found such speculation profitable
And now he is a grandfather
Still vigorous, still working
At the dynamic center of a successful life

IV. The Best Way Out Is Always Through

"Len says one steady pull more ought to do it.

He says the best way out is always through."

Robert Frost, "A Servant to Servants" in
North of Boston

Maria Callas Tames La Scala—4/9/1958

I am in the wings
In moments I will be queen once more
Will discipline my subjects with the heat of their own desires

I could perform nearly any part
A rude wooden bucket
I let a new character spill into me
From the spring of the composer's score
A tranquil liquid
But when it pours from me again, I am in it

Our rehearsals are only our descents through waterways
The furrows, channels, pools, flumes, marshes, and shallows
Down to the performing sea
But I have discovered that some characters fall reliably through
chasms
And always culminate in ocean storms
The waves of their performances threaten the audience with an
unendurable forcefulness
Lady Macbeth, Norma, Medea
These were the composers' challenges to their god
Breaking taboos, soliciting judgment
And these I choose as my challenges to my audience
No longer the lyrical soprano they once came to revere
But the evil they now come to exorcise
And I am consumed with the power and guilt

They sense too that I am leaving them
And they are enraged
They want me to go on with this illicit love affair

With my audience
Which I initiated
For which they reward me
But I can feel the night air around me
Recall the red flower
That captured my heart on my way to rehearsal
One spring morning long, long ago
When I returned at twilight
It had been picked, my flower
And I never had any joy of it
So red in the spring morning

Will they respond tonight to my wiles, my gestures, my trills
Or will my audience lynch me, quite unceremoniously
Right here on stage
For on my best nights they sometimes hiss, those snakes that I charm
And on my worst nights they have cheered me until I was deeply
                                        ashamed
I am not the mistress I once was
This challenge I once craved, carved and enkindled
No longer possesses me
I cannot concentrate at rehearsals; my voice cracks now with anxiety
                                        and softens with desire

I cannot go on tonight
I am no queen, only a child
I have no desire to be beheaded

But should someone push me sharply from behind
I will I have no doubt still plunge, violently, to my destiny

Be True

1

On our way out of town

As we had often said we would

We stopped by a field

As Frost did by woods

And got out to look

The tree stood alone in the distance

And we walked out toward it

Glorious, capacious as the day

Limbs spread, rustling, rooted

Open to earth, wind, and sky

Absolutely itself

With nothing to distort or encroach

In harmony with worm, bird

And nitrogen fixing bacteria

Magnetic, majestic

Beautiful as a rainbow

As a sunrise

Then, back in the car

Anita and I dissected idiosyncrasies

Of old friends

Felicities, incongruities, grotesqueries

In particular how many

Had chosen to vanish

And wondered if any of those

Would be among the attendees

2

If we had not met long before
But come to talk for the first time
At that 35th reunion
We would not have hit it off
Would not have had much to say
To one another
But in school we were close friends
We could never have been lovers
But might back then
Have enjoyed being neighbors
Lab partners, even roommates
We once spent a day together in Santa Cruz
Where she'd gone to college
Rode the merry-go-round
Visited the botanical garden
And from time to time
We talked late into the night
Shared confidences
We both trained in England senior year
And I left her the car, a Wolseley, I'd bought for £200

3

Here's some of what I retain of what she shared
More than forty years ago:
An enviable affluent San Francisco childhood
Nob Hill manse, substantial father
Lovely accomplished mother
Salty older sister

(Later contentedly married
To a father-aged husband)
And a winsome younger sister
High school graduation
(Or was it the prom?)
At the Emeryville Hyatt
College in Santa Cruz
Torn I see now
Between the old San Francisco aristocracy
And counterculture freedom and equality
Coming down hard at school for the latter
Before embarking on a melancholy, long retreat
And with a vague growing foundational despondency
Was there a death or two?
Father? Mother? Both?

4

Of course, we were younger then
And the world was coarser, brighter
Pregnant with threat and violence
During the first year she more sang than spoke
Like a sparrow
In short liquid bursts of news and enthusiasm
Never from a distant branch
Always alive, close by, and present in the moment
A deep, conspiratorial laugh
Aspirational syntax
A semantics of possibility and promise
Boyish, shy and forceful all at once
Then she moved in with a sweet, immature classmate

And, losing some of the urgency and emphasis
Turned, for a time, peevish and superficial
Though never foolish
A quiet pool
In which you could still
Apparently
See to the bottom

5

Things got stormy in the clinical years
The stress, the travel
The loneliness of being single again
Fed a cruel, sudden anguish
That she might never find the right partner
Might end unloved
It was a dark, cold, snowless winter in Bath
And her confidence, for once, failed her
My one visit was, unsurprisingly, little comfort
But then, on the flight back from England
She met an older man, wealthy, never married
A scold and forceful raconteur
We heard her many qualms about him
She asked us all what we thought
(A sure sign she had made up her mind)
And they were married soon after graduation

6

Of the three or four days we spent with them
On Long Island, my wife and I

Some five or ten years later
I recall a composite summer's day
Green leafy yard, tea and cakes
A young precocious spoiled daughter
Vehement advice about finance
(He rose early each morning
To trade overseas for an hour or two)
What brand of soap to buy
Where to travel, what to eat
And exclusive regional histories
Of companies and people
"We live just down the street from P.G. Wodehouse"
She echoing and amplifying
His comments and judgments
Taking direction
A faint echo of the voice I knew
A shy ghost in the middle of the day
And then they stopped responding
Presumably something we said or did
Or didn't
In some esoteric language or protocol
We hadn't yet (now probably never will) learned

7

We have since grown more familiar
With the down-the-street syndrome
As you've read, one friend bought down the street from Stephen
King
Another from Angie Dickinson
My father's best friend's son

A successful TV producer
Found himself down the street
From my best friend's brother, a screenwriter
What they mean to convey is less who they're near
Than how far away they're getting from us
Since wealth, like the past, heaven, music
Is another country
(And fame yet another, yet more remote)
Requires passport, visa, foreign tongue
Demanding, that is, of us
Things we were either not willing
Or not able flawlessly to acquire

8

So what's new? I asked
Well, I'm alone again
G. died two years ago
And J.'s off at college
And have you been working?
Insurance physicals
From time to time over the years
But now I've gone back to school
Georgetown Law
I'm about to start a foundation
To address malpractice
It's never been done properly
I think we can unravel the crisis
Let me tell you how
It was not that she never used her license
To benefit people

Nor that she
Who'd never experienced the threat
Thought she could *solve* malpractice
I'd have forgiven her more than that
As she was when we'd first met
But faced with a wall of aristocratic arrogance
Condescension, vehemence, certainty
I could find no way back into that past

9

It was much worse like this
Had we simply not hit it off
There'd have been nothing lost
We'd have gone our indifferent separate ways
But we missed one another as we'd been
And were mutually appalled
She by my weakness and gullibility
I by her cynical world-weariness
But there was something far worse
She'd become downright vulpine
A transformation I'd only seen twice before
Once in a high school classmate
Who'd performed for the foreign service and the CIA
And once in a plastic surgeon
At an earlier medical school reunion
Their features were as different as frog from elephant from kangaroo
But they were all plethoric
Brick red, dissipated,
Their faces at rest distorted
By anger and cruelty
Ravenous, superior, lonely

A third of those who have alcohol
Three or more times a day
Become cirrhotic
A fifth of those who smoke
Contract chronic obstructive lung disease
It's only a theory, but I suspect
At least a fifth of those who acquire a fortune
Say a net worth of $5 million
Suffer from affluenza
Become vulpine or arrogant or pretentious
A small dose of G., we found
Could be bracing
But day in day out for twenty years
Might cloy
I became convinced that what we'd gone to
Should not be called reunion
But reconsideration, reexamination, revision, even judgment day
Because people metamorphose
And lives can not only drift but can accelerate apart

11

I couldn't formulate my thoughts
Until I shared them aloud to Anita
On the way back
A person rarely grows alone in a field like that tree
The world is so much with us
Pressing close, arguing, falsifying
Cornering the light, siphoning the water

Exacting patience, resilience, ingenuity
Or
A new persona
Short cuts, self-assertion, loss
Life tapers to a simple yes or no
And what makes us human
Is that this becomes a real choice
That we can say no
Or "only if you behave"
To matter, life, the universe
Our own atoms, cells and molecules
Hopes, dreams, dispositions
Of course at a cost
Or say yes
And grow as close to what we would be
In an open field
As makes neither novelty nor fantasy nor decrement

Unconditional

Glint of metal, man threat
Woman screaming
Central Park, evening
He, on his way
Home from work
Scales a boundary wall
Wrestles away the knife
Calms with earnest speech
Leaves them behind
Tended by osmotically bold
Rebound bystanders

(The next week
Same place
Same time
Same scene enacted
Same players
This time
He walks on past)

That is what, about him
We all tell first
Next his running blocks
To (red light) overtake a car
And return a purse
The driver had left
On her trunk

But to me
What was most compelling

About Frank's best friend
(As about Frank himself)
Was more fundamental
Than do-good intervention:
That wellspring, that fountain
Of kindness overflowing
Inundating his vicinity
With that optimistic, generous
Conviction of goodness
Rightness, possibility
In whoever stood before him
In people, in mankind
Rooted
Unshakeable

"As when a woman
Beautiful, fancy free
Going by, turns heads
They were like magnets
Both of them
Majestically humble
They drew after them
Hopes and dreams
Loves and wishes

Like clematis in summer
Or camellia in winter
Like bare cherry branches
Force-bloomed in indoor vases
They were both profuse
In nonstop flower
Everyone, *we all*

Wanted to be near them
Exult in their colors
Stealthily pick a flower
All our own
It was a privilege to spend
With either of them
An hour, an evening"

"Best friends?
Hardly
They barely talked
Once Steve moved to Boston
Though it couldn't have
Been just the distance
Only four hours
Something happened
Between them
Don't you think
And aren't you two
Being a little hoity-toity
Sure, they were both
Nice and kind
But still people
Sometimes irritable
Sometimes foolish
Different from one another

Frank, at least
Could be busy
Set limits
Had some iron in him
He didn't let swindlers

Get away with much
He was kind
And he was fair
But he was objective, moral
Had expectations
The other—less"

"Still they both
(Absent confidence?)
Married early
And happily
Lived first
In the same building
Then mere blocks apart
In the Bronx

And their sons
Remember
They had the first two
In our crowd
We all had to hold them
So lovely
So bright
So much promise
'Nature's answer to Hitler'
We used to say
Still, later

Something clearly did go wrong
With Steve's kids at least
They somehow lacked buoyancy
Never found their way

I always wondered why
Nicest men I ever met
Steve and Frank"

"See, that's what I was saying
They grew apart
And love
At least the unconditional kind
Is overrated
'Listen kid,' Frank's Jane
(My best friend
I do know from best friends)
Used to say
And I knew
Though childless myself then
(Learned the hard way since again)
She was right to be tough
To chasten them
Mold them, hold them accountable
We all need expectations
Adversity
Maybe Steve's brood
Had too little
His Bess was too soft
Too nurtury
Next thing you know
There were cults
Alcohol
Refusals to finish school
To work for someone else
Then came the poor choices
Broken hearts

Broken promises
Marriages
Lives
Steve was
I can say it now
Even more beautiful than Frank
A fabulous friend
But a terrible father
I'd like to be wrong
So please
Tell me
How else to explain it"

"Genes, chance, peers
Bess' death at forty
Take, on my block
In childhood
The Blairs
Nine sons
Eight dropouts
And one a neurosurgeon
There was nothing
Wrong with Steve
He struggled
Every day to cheer
Each person he met
Left the world
Far better than he found it

Something beautiful
Something we didn't fully understand
Died with the two of them

Maybe it was his children
He was wonderful
With other people's children"

"Maybe so
But these are facts
They both had three kids
Frank's all did well
Steve's all did not
Science aside
You all know
In your hearts
Much as we loved him
Steve got that
At least a little
Wrong
That's how it looks to me
Metal, scream"

Poems oversimplify
It was
Always is
More complicated
Than these old friends
Suggest
Steve married twice
His second wife had a son
By a short prior marriage
So Steve brought up
A fourth child
From the age of five
Who had more worldly success

(But less of his benevolence)
Than any
Of the crowd's other children
And the third child
Conceived with the second wife
Had sufficient resilience
Made a satisfactory life

Though the conflict
And its parsing
Does remain
As stark and problematic
As they proposed

Were they best friends?
How/when/where did they meet?
What, if anything
Estranged them?
What did they do in the war?
We never asked
Now no one alive seems to know

Humming Bard

The humming bard is a genius
Not of song but of movement
Does what no other bird can

Hovers, rises
Flies backwards
Upside down

Bullets across the field
Of vision
Like science/fiction

A thing of spongy bone
Flesh, more than a thousand feathers
Heart beat twenty times the rate of ours

Smaller than a plum
Contending with the possible
The universe

As dazzling, patient and comprehensive
As Homer or Chaucer
Master of all we survey

Mental Still Lives

1

In our mental still lives
It was year round sunny
Cool, chiming, sea-breezy
White and sparkling
Too special to soil by mere daily living
Sharing a remote earthquake risk
With the rest of the Bay Area
But otherwise halcyon, Olympian
We decided it would do no harm
A week in Santa Cruz

2

We booked for February
Had a modest history there and friends
Arranged hotel, restaurants
A visit to Carmel Village
Another to Half Moon Bay
But the heaviest snow in ten years
Closed the passes
We couldn't get to the grocery store
Much less to California
It had grown yet more remote, more special

3

Still we were resilient
Faute-de-mieuxed in May
It had been, we were told
An unseasonable year
Rained two days out of three
It stayed so for us
We gravitated to North Cliff Drive
Watched the surfers
Acquired two country French tablecloths
(Clean-lined linen
Flowery purple and green designs
We've used in our dining room ever since)
On the way to Capitola
Ate out, of course, had ice cream
Visited two adjacent redwood state parks
And the Marine Discovery Center
But not our old haunts
Not the Boardwalk (no lingering attraction)
Nor the Botanical Garden
(Recent thefts
And the police screening visitors)
We noticed, but discounted, the darkness filtering in

4

The highlight was lunch on the Municipal Wharf
With Myrna and Badi
Mely and Vic
Anita's college classmates and their partners

Enough variety and distraction
Bustle, menus, gossip, and wit
Birds, fish, shops, tides
And a post-meal pilgrimage to Mely's son Jonathan and family
In the hills above the city
Just forty-five minutes from the restaurant
A unique private retreat

5

When Jonathan was fourteen
He'd visited us with his mother in Holyoke, MA
Swum in our pool, slept in the house
Had fond memories
At loose ends in the turmoil
Of our visit
He chose to talk with me
About his successes at work
The purchase of the property
His work on the house

6

The house had belonged to a failing religious cult
Riven by dissension and poor husbandry
And conflicted about the sale
It was hard even to schedule a visit
The place was filthy
Rooms were arbitrarily subdivided by makeshift walls
Still he persisted: it was a salvageable and an imposing site

And his older brother owned a house
Just uphill across the road
He was nearly two years wrangling
But he did in the end take title

7

He didn't mind the work
He could just manage the expense
Mornings and evenings
On weekends, during vacations
He'd remade the place
It was enviably lovely
The family had accommodated
Living around the construction
And was now beginning to reap its reward
There was a glorious view looking west toward San Jose
The interior all blond wood and sunlight
State of the art California contemporary
Yet with a rough, homemade feel
We talked at a table in the palatial kitchen
Spacious, all the best appliances
A discretionary island
Utensils hanging from the ceiling

8

There was still the downstairs to address, he said
The wood floors, special order
Took months to lay

But he could now see daylight
Proud and cheerful, he was also self-effacing
"Anyone could do this, who sets his mind to it"
(Not I)
Already he could accommodate his mother's memorabilia
And he was building her her own house to retire in
Right there on the property
He took us on a tour
The whole family came along
Then we drove back to Santa Cruz and next day back home
The house on the hillside receded
Another mental still life

9

On Friday the story started to lose its symmetry
We heard that Jonathan and his brother
Had been force to evacuate at two the previous morning
They were not the first of our friends
To experience this new California amenity
Dick and Joan, in their late 80s
Were evacuated from their home
On Tubbs Lane in Calistoga two years ago
During the Tubbs fire
They stayed two days with friends
Before returning home

10

But two nights later
We heard that all three houses had burned to the ground

"I had just finished the last floor, auntie"
Jonathan said
I have so far failed
To create a mental still life
To accommodate this event
Fire and the previous image
Being for me incompatible
Perhaps it is magical thinking
That if I cannot picture the episode
It won't have happened
And I won't have to do the hard work
Of mourning Jonathan's loss
And our planet's
These nails in the heart of all our plans for any meaningful future

11

They didn't die
Can start again
All their memories
And Mely's
Out of the world now, just in their minds
Chastened, annealed, fortified
But intact
If there is to be a future
It will rest, at least in part, upon them
And on all the other victims of the changes we've wrought
Our global warming
Our famines and fires
Our storms and pandemics
Our corruptions and inequalities

Will depend upon their resilience, forgiveness, and creativity
And our willingness to improve
Santa Cruz now for us, like New Orleans
A diminished mental still life
Or more accurately, two superimposed dissonant still lives
No longer a physical place to which we ever wish to return

A Singular Loyalty

For Kay Ganz

Perhaps it was my helplessness in early childhood
The naked pain and fear
Or that I became in time, in some small way, a writer
That I was your best friend's son
The first child of the next generation
First in your circle of friends
That you have always valued loyalty
The feeling, intent, and responsibility

Something that dates from, recalls
Manhattan when it was a down-to-earth fit place to live
When a butcher and his family could live comfortably in Washington
Heights
When Hunter and City Colleges were national treasures
When teenage girls could safely walk in Riverside Park at sunset
When, before and after the Second World War
All was deadly serious, threat then promise
Or really both together

Perhaps it was the nature of life on Long Island in the '50s and '60s
Neighbor helping neighbor
All the neighborhood children drifting together after stickball
For cookies and lemonade into any house on the block
One suburb melting into the next
Levittowns, Peyton Places
Routine, hope, and squalor
Everything growing, new trees, new lives, new communities

* *

Whatever it was it has lasted now both our lifetimes
A letter each year at the winter equinox
A card every year on my birthday
News of our families, the state of each universe, each mind
While to the uninitiate this might seem simple acquaintance,
                                        shallow
The subtext has always been, unsullied by trial:
Should it become necessary
You would take me in like family, I you, whatever the cost

And that has been a buoy, helped us prosper
Even when unmindful, between exchanges
On a plane prior to, parallel to family
This improbable attachment, appreciative, discreet,
Arising from such poor soil
Still green and unconditional, when many closer ties have withered
Even now in your eighties
Yet virtual and, until this, unspoken

The Heron Shows Us How

The heron stands in shallow water
Like an aging conductor
On the podium before a concert
His concentration as total and relaxed
As tension can ever be
And he watches
Whether the water or the horizon
Without moving, without wishing
A Buddhist in the depths of a meditation
That has apparently no goal or end
His sustenance is his vigil
His ground his field
The concert will not begin for us
He hears it playing in and around him
And it makes him stiller yet

Reminiscence

He was perhaps shy
Or maybe felt an instinctive restraint
"Children should enjoy a protected but unsuperintended childhood"
Stayed in the background
Could have been mistaken by the unobservant
For a mere bystander

But he was a suburban household Hephaestus
The architect of a substantial part of our childhood
Finished the basement and furnished the pool table
Extended the playroom and added the screens and windows
(And paid for the comic books)
Provided the pool and picnic table
Where our social life grew and prospered
His workshop and tool belt
His forge and anvil

And not just the physical architecture
He parleyed his long commute and longer workdays
Into an illusion of affluence
Spread out a cornucopia of food and fun
Opened his novel palace to the less fortunate
Defined comfort for us
Unassuming
Consequential
Kind, quiet, and, later, sentimental

More than anyone we knew
He embodied what America was then
And should have remained

He did more with less
And had more impact more selflessly
Than anyone who abutted our carefree youth

A Nail

1

He will say
I was competitive, ambitious and unrelenting
That I hated to lose
Was loud, difficult
Handsome, smart
Loyal and driven
Promising
But hard to pin down
And he'll be right
As far as that can take you
But all that you could see in my face
Hear in my voice
After a day in my company

But I was also a withholder
From wisdom or policy or fear
Never revealed what I felt or why
My motives, in any case, helplessly diverse
Wracked with more conflict than a courtroom
Or a hurricane
Hemorrhaging conflict
Thriving on it

Oh I did let him visit
Just him, not the others
Sit at our kitchen table
And examine first hand
The family dynamics

But I don't think he could truly see
The inferno of arrogance, aggression, and contempt
Behind the welcoming façade
The suffocating intimacy
He recapped with platitudes
Seemed to think it all just an intensified version
Of his own family's dinner table palaver
No way different in kind
But they were only play acting, defanged
Only halfway to any consequence in the real world

2

What I was in his world
The one I'd chosen
Was tempered by what I had to be
In the one I was born into
Where fired, fixed, programmed, and armed
I might have been robot or missile

It was an odd surrogate family
Bourgeois, saccharine, Jewish, sophomoric
Traits I loathed or scorned
(My father an activist union steward)
I couldn't bring myself to read the comics
Couldn't stomach playing pool
Or swimming in the pool
But ping-pong and Risk and cards and debating
Were compensation
And junior high offered no better option

3

I did love that chosen family
Whole afternoons of ping-pong in the basement with him
Just about evenly matched
Elemental
He defense, I offense
Anger, hope, misery, triumph
Everything right there on the tabletop
A trial without the posturing, the verbiage
Money-where-the-mouth-is competition
No quarter asked or given

And arguments among the four of us
Exploratory oratory
Agitated as bees in a jar
But it wasn't just love
I was also envious and contemptuous
They were so innocent, brittle, and ineffectual
Optimistic and beautiful
I wanted their buoyancy
And mocked it

4

Let's start again
They all wear glasses
(Well he doesn't actually wear his
Not even for sports
From vanity? Deprecation?
How can he be so good without?

Would he be better with?)
Anyway they see the world mediated
Through lenses
Rose-colored? Spectral?
(Saw the world
All this is decades ago)
Not in its fullness
But pruned of threat and promise
Lose (lost) much of their energy
Riding bicycles, daydreaming their soft-focus dreams
About love, money, fortune, family, fame
Weaving improbable futures nightly
On a phantom loom
Starting over fresh and empty each next morning
Never out in the day, working, building

I took no part in any of that
Didn't have time for it
Nor for girls then either
Consumed by what seemed prodigious destinies and missions
What they read or imagined, I did
Kept company with the principal
Shipped out one summer on a tramp steamer

But for a while we
He and I anyway
Were inseparable
Distinctive equals
Met almost daily
At school, at sports, at odds
Our visions of life fruitfully clashing
Like cymbals or syllables

Proclaiming diverse channels to difference
Shedding splendor like confetti
As do all things strictly controlled
Or utterly free of control
Or especially the two in conflict
Never worked together
Two oxen in harness
For a common good

5

And then it was suddenly over
We were dispersed
In colleges across the Northeast
Hours, and milieux, apart
And if I missed it (them)
The missing was easy to bear
Substitute for
Soon forgotten
Even the best families have a use-by date
From consumption by their trivial trial world
They were forced now to live and act
In the larger one I'd always inhabited
Our booster rockets fell away

What a cliché
Two became doctors, two lawyers
One failed life; three shared their affluence
With loving stable partners
Two had children
But attempts to reconnect

175

Well-intentioned
Failed
We did not know what mattered any longer
How to praise or promote or protect one another
Didn't need to succeed
Had sounder alternatives
Had moved on

6

I am confident he will one day write about me
Though the relationship was not decisive
It was consuming
Disturbing
Unresolved
Just ended
I don't think he ever competed with me
As I with him
Turmoil there only a path to concord
He will probably soften my edges
Whitewash my motives
And lament our failure to reconnect
Never understand
My refusal to respond
To his overtures

But I no longer want to interrogate or understand
I burn my bridges
And dwellings and communities
And live at the top
Upon ashes and historical detritus

176

Supported by former families
Former conflicts
Former environments
My new life, new community
Buoyed upon decomposition
On the garbage dump
Of my former lives and loves and beliefs
I have always been brutal, callous, impervious
He could not understand that
Never did

Acknowledgments:
Prior Publications

"Dumb Blonde" and "Be True" in *Adelaide Review*

"Unconditional" in *Praxis*, June 19, 2020

"The Heron Shows Us How" in *Sheila-Na-Gig*; "An Insect Aside" in *Fictional Café*.

About Atmosphere Press

Founded in 2015, Atmosphere Press was built on the principles of Honesty, Transparency, Professionalism, Kindness, and Making Your Book Awesome. As an ethical and author-friendly hybrid press, we stay true to that founding mission today.

If you're a reader, enter our giveaway for a free book here:

SCAN TO ENTER
BOOK GIVEAWAY

If you're a writer, submit your manuscript for consideration here:

SCAN TO SUBMIT
MANUSCRIPT

And always feel free to visit Atmosphere Press and our authors online at atmospherepress.com. See you there soon!

About the Author

ALAN COHEN'S first publication as a poet was in the PTA news-letter when he was ten years old. He graduated from Farmingdale High School, where he was Poetry Editor of the magazine *The Bard*. He earned a BA in English from Vassar College and attended the University of California at Davis Medical School. He completed his internship in Boston and his residency in Hawaii. Alan then served as a Primary Care physician, teacher, and Chief of Primary Care at the VA, first in Fresno, CA, and later in Roseburg, OR. He has continued to write both medical and literary articles; over the years, he has had letters to the editor published in *Poetry* and *The New Yorker* and has been published in the *American Journal of Medicine* and the *New England Journal of Medicine*. In the past two years, he has had 182 poems published in ninety venues.